Praise for
Raising Multiracial Children

"*Raising Multiracial Children* is an indispensable study that illustrates the importance of speaking with children on race so that they can be prepared to deal with the reality of it throughout their lives. Nayani uses accessible language to weave together terminology, anecdotes, classroom activities, recommended resources, and her own experiences as a multiethnic woman, mother, and educator to provide clear insight on how to have a meaningful conversation on race and multiracial identities. It is a vital book for parents, caregivers, and educators committed to this kind of work. Bravo!"

—RUDY P. GUEVARRA JR., author of
*Becoming Mexipino: Multiethnic Identities
and Communities in San Diego*

"Far too often, race is examined and discussed along a Black and White binary, which leaves multiracial children feeling as though they do not have a place at the table. In order to strive for racial inclusion and justice, our conversations must include the nuances of multiracial identity."

—LIZ KLEINROCK, educator and founder of
Teach and Transform

"*Raising Multiracial Children* is an excellent resource for parents, teachers, family members, and friends of the increasing number of multiracial children. It provides exercises, questions, an intersectional analysis, resources, curricula, and lots of examples of age-appropriate guidelines—a veritable toolbox of resources—for nurturing and supporting the next generation of multiracial people and their allies. Farzana Nayani writes with caring, personal experience, and deep insight, illustrating her examples with moving personal stories from multiracial young people and adults."

—PAUL KIVEL, educator, activist, and author
of *Uprooting Racism: How White People Can
Work for Racial Justice*

"My wife is Indian, born in New Delhi, and I am African American, born in the American South. Our three children—the 'Three Little Blindians'—are growing up in Los Angeles with a vastly different experience than either of us had. On my wife's side of the family tree, our children can trace their roots back to the founding of New Delhi. On my side, we're aware of a few proud generations, and we've also had to find joy in discovering our African roots together. We've done our best to teach them that they are not 'half' anything. Rather, they have two rich ancestries that they can call on to ground them in their journey through life. As we have experienced in our own Black and Indian family, raising multiracial children is such a critical topic. Farzana isolates invaluable tools to help give any child a more comprehensive sense of self-identity."

—JASON GEORGE, actor from *Grey's Anatomy*
and *Station 19*, on raising children with his
wife, writer and educator Vandana Khanna

"I can't imagine a person more qualified to write about multiracial and multicultural children than Farzana Nayani. She presents excellent advice to parents, teachers, and cross-cultural trainers concerning the challenges and opportunities faced by multiracial children. She brings a rich background to this task based on years of careful study, knowledge learned from leading workshops, and her own experiences as a spouse and mother."

—RICHARD W. BRISLIN, professor emeritus,
University of Hawai`i

"A book like this one is critical to our united humanity. Whether we are teachers, parents, or friends, we all need tools to help the children in our lives cultivate their identity – not as we or society see it or want it to be, but with regards to how they see it and need it to be. Ms. Nayani's book guides us in the consideration of those tools, and in our efforts to apply those tools in helping us grow and helping children grow."

—VELINA HASU HOUSTON, MFA, PhD,
playwright and distinguished professor

Raising
Multiracial
Children

Raising Multiracial Children

Tools for Nurturing Identity in a Racialized World

FARZANA NAYANI

Foreword by Dr. Paul Spickard

Afterword by Dr. Velina Hasu Houston

North Atlantic Books
Berkeley, California

Published by
North Atlantic Books
Berkeley, California

Cover art and design by Jess Morphew
Book design by Happenstance Type-O-Rama

Printed in Canada

Raising Multiracial Children: Tools for Nurturing Identity in a Racialized World is sponsored and published by the Society for the Study of Native Arts and Sciences (dba North Atlantic Books), an educational nonprofit based in Berkeley, California, that collaborates with partners to develop cross-cultural perspectives, nurture holistic views of art, science, the humanities, and healing, and seed personal and global transformation by publishing work on the relationship of body, spirit, and nature.

North Atlantic Books' publications are available through most bookstores. For further information, visit our website at www.northatlanticbooks.com or call 800-733-3000.

Library of Congress Cataloging-in-Publication data
is available from the publisher upon request.

1 2 3 4 5 6 7 8 9 MARQUIS 25 24 23 22 21 20

For all the multiracial
children of the world,
including my dear
Zakri and Zain

Contents

Foreword

FARZANA NAYANI CHANGES LIVES and human relationships. For the last couple of decades, she has been working with the people who inhabit corporations, universities, schools, and governmental agencies to help them get better at creating and managing multicultural settings and populations. Much of her work has a special focus on multiracial identity. The number of multiracial families and individuals has skyrocketed over the past couple of decades, and Farzana Nayani has been there to help us cope with our new reality.

It is often noted that many if not most Black and Brown parents give their children, especially their sons, various versions of The Talk. As the children come of age and gain social awareness, their parents let them know that they will be racialized in the public eye. They help their children develop strategies (albeit sometimes humiliating ones) for dealing with teachers, police, and other strangers who may fear them or think ill of them and so treat them badly. It is an unfortunate truth that in a deeply racist society, children of color need to be taught how to cope with everyday racism.

Now, in *Raising Multiracial Children*, Farzana Nayani gives us another talk, one that we need. This is The Talk for parents of multiracial children, for teachers and others who work closely with multiracial children, and also for society at large. Farzana says that we need to make space for multiracial people, and then she helps us learn how to do that. She tells us who multiracial people are and suggests ways of thinking about them and talking about them. She draws on insights from sociology, psychology, family therapy, social work, and other helping disciplines. She challenges us to engage directly, and appropriately, with race talk. She helps us see both the rigidity and the fluidity that may characterize racial identities. She engages questions of racial authenticity, racial performance, and colorism. She points out that racial identities are products both of external social imposition and personal choice and expression, and challenges us to lay our loyalty on the side of the individual.

Nayani charts the course of racial identity development and sorts out the ways that multiracial people often navigate their identity journey. She points to the pitfalls that often await multiracial people as they negotiate their space in society. I especially like chapter 5, which lays out common issues that multiracial children face as they grow to maturity—mainly judgmental impositions by monoracial people who would be gatekeepers—and strategies for coping with those hurdles. She has a great chapter for teachers, with lots of ideas for things they can do in the classroom. She follows her multiracial subjects through to adulthood—to college, and into their careers—with helpful advice all along the way. Finally, Nayani ends with a call to multiracial community-building and social activism.

Along the way, Nayani offers us a ton of good advice. Don't try to ignore race. It's not going away, so talk about it (and she gives some strategies for doing so). Don't fractionate when you refer to a multiracial person. Don't assume what their identity must be—observe, listen, and let them reveal themselves to you. Don't give in to those who would enforce their racial choices on you. Be wary of DNA ancestry testing. And so on and on.

Nayani also gives concrete suggestions for parents and teachers about questions they can pose, conversations they can have, and activities they can sponsor to help multiracial children sort out their identity issues. The last third of the book is a treasure trove of resources that parents, teachers, and multiracial individuals themselves can call on.

I wish that I had had this book when I was raising my five multiracial children. Had I read it then, I would have been a better parent. I am so glad that they now have *Raising Multiracial Children* to help them bring up my multiracial grandchildren.

> —PAUL SPICKARD, PhD, distinguished professor of history, affiliate professor of Asian American studies, Black studies, Chicana/o studies, East Asian studies, and religious studies at the University of California, Santa Barbara; author of *Race in Mind: Critical Essays;* and coeditor of *Red and Yellow, Black and Brown: Decentering Whiteness in Mixed Race Studies* and *Global Mixed Race*

Acknowledgments

I'D FIRSTLY LIKE to acknowledge the Tongva peoples on whose land I currently reside and where most of this book was written, the xʷməθkʷəy̓əm (Musqueam) and all Coast Salish peoples upon whose land I was raised, and the Kānaka ʻōiwi or Kānaka maoli of the islands of Hawaiʻi whose ʻaina (land) I had settled on, as it is within all of these places that I have formed much of my existence.

This book is dedicated to all who are devoted to advancing inclusion, belonging, and understanding for multiracial children and their families. My coming into contact with the lives and stories of multiracial individuals over many years has borne the need to address this specific topic directly. As a multiethnic individual who is an educator, community advocate, and parent of multiracial children, it is critical for me to create a work which serves as a resource for caretakers of youth, from these variety of perspectives. As such, I feel it is important to combine theory, practice, and lived experience for a comprehensive, holistic look at these issues.

I have witnessed fantastic work on multiracial identity siloed in the realms that they thrive in—from popular news, to academia, blogging, film, visual and performing arts, and community events. This book endeavors to bring these vantage points together in a cohesive work that centers the experiences and needs of multiracial individuals as we journey to explore the greater concepts of identity and racialization in the world today. I am indebted to those who have contributed to the conversation about the multiracial experience before me. This work stands on the bedrock created by those efforts. My deepest gratitude to all of these makers, creators, scholars, writers, artists, activists, organizers, and visionaries, as well as those who plan to take up the mantle to continue this work in the future. I am also thankful and humbled by the outpouring of support and responses by multiracial individuals and families who responded to my call for stories and experiences. It is for you that this book is written, and because of your triumphs and expressions of your lived experiences that we are able to have this conversation today.

I have many people to thank who have impacted me over the years through their presence and commitment to the multiracial movement, activism, and education:

Dr. Maria P. P. Root, Dr. Paul Spickard, Dr. Velina Hasu Houston, Dr. Curtiss Takada-Rooks, Kip Fulbeck, Dr. Rudy P. Guevarra Jr., Dr. Laura Kina, Ken Tanabe, Fanshen Cox, Dr. Kelly F. Jackson, Louie Gong, Dr. Lily Anne Welty Tamai, Edward Sumoto, Jeff Chiba Stearns, Rasmia Kirmani, Dr. Rika Houston, Duncan Ryūken Williams, Rasheda Carroll, and Janet Stickmon. You have in one way or another touched my life or have been models whom I look to both as guides and colleagues, as well as the voice for the multiracial community.

I'd like to specially thank my colleagues at the Multiracial Americans of Southern California (MASC) who I consider to be my chosen multiracial family and who embody dedication, steadfastness, and community: Nancy Brown, Thomas Lopez, Dr. Jennifer Noble, Sonia Smith-Kang, Dr. Laurel Hoa, Athena Asklipaidis, Delia Douglas-Haight, Thomas Elliott, Erica Wall, Kiyoshi Houston, Larissa Chiari-Keith, Sandi Tamkin. My creative friends and talented colleagues who live the mixed race experience, have lent an ear, artistic eye, and research to this conversation, and have been a source of continual support: Diyana Mendoza-Price, Alexander Pryor, Lisa Strack, Rahimeh Ramezany, Erika Bertling, and Shaiyanne Dar. Noah Balch, the protector and my trusted advisor. My friends and colleagues from the intercultural and diversity and inclusion fields who are or have been a strong presence in my life, consistently offering dialogue, affirmation, and inspiration: Mary Farmer, Leila Buck, Kelli McLoud-Schingen, Carmen White Janak, Tamara Cherie Thorpe, Patricia Coleman, Brett Parry, Valli Murphy, Sue Shinomiya, Dr. Joel Brown, Dr. Amer F. Ahmed, Farah Bala, Stacey Gordon, Sonya Kaleel, Natasha Aruliah, Indy Batth, Parker Johnson, Dr. Shakti Butler, Dr. Sumi Pendakur, Jade Agua, Kesa Kivel, and Murray Mann. My lifelong academic advisors: Dr. Richard W. Brislin, Dr. Gary Fontaine, the late Dr. Paul B. Pedersen, the late Dr. Gabriele Helms, and Dr. Patricia E. Halagao. My healers and teachers, who have kept me steadfast on the path of my authentic self: Dr. Jennifer Lisa Vest, Heather Rebecca Wilson, Dr. Kate Siner, Katrina Long, Dr. Gulrukh Bala.

Much appreciation goes to the staff at North Atlantic Books who were exceptional partners throughout the entire publishing process, from vision, to design, to print. It is because of their relentless commitment to tell this story that this book came to be. My recognition and gratitude to Shayna Keyles, Ebonie Ledbetter, Adrienne Armstrong, Emily Boyd, Julia Sadowski, and Bevin Donahue, whose unwavering dedication, insights, and amazing team effort have brought my words to life. To former NAB staff Vanessa Ta, Pamela Berkman, and Christina Dedios, who were instrumental in guiding this idea from its inception and eased me into the world of publishing. A special thanks to Tim McKee, who offered invaluable input throughout this journey of writing, and whose insights and dialogue have moved me to realize this project.

I could not have completed this work without the support of my entire family, including my parents and sister, who have led me to be me who I am today, and whose imagination for the possibilities of my life were limitless. My soul friends whose decades of friendship bring joy and meaning to my life: Shazeen Kassam, Sarah Janmohamed, Aliya Dhanani, Feriyal Amal Aslam, Theresa Scott, Paul Wong, Salim Hirji, Ferial Qamar, Pamela Ireland, Charles Babb, and Anisa Kassim. The Dar family, my hānai family who I deeply admire and could never have dreamed I would have found, and whose open-heartedness and generosity of spirit is a role model for so many others. My dear children, Zakri and Zain, who are my foundation and strength in all that I do, and whose overflowing love and earnestness fuel my perseverance. To my beloved husband and partner, Shafiq: our two families coming together has been a treasure, and the birth of our own children has enriched my life with even deeper purpose. Your untiring support and sweet encouragement have kept me going, even in times of doubt or moments where I have felt lost, on the wrong track, or seemingly directionless. It is with the continuing determination to create a world that can hold all aspects of our lives and the lives of those around us that keeps me grounded and able to continue this work and strive toward a vision of a greater reality for us all. I am truly honored to be on this path with you and am eager for our next adventures.

In my consulting work as a diversity, equity, and inclusion specialist and in my coaching work as an intuitive healer, I do not and cannot start any conversation without firstly honoring our ancestors and secondly exploring the identities of each participant, being mindful of those who did not have access to be in the room or the ability to reflect on this moment. It is essential to connect the historical, spiritual, and ancestral lineage of us as people with an understanding of our own current identities, as I truly believe this holds the keys to lasting empathy, which is the underpinning for true inclusion, intercultural understanding, equity, justice, healing, and societal change.

This all begins with our children.

Introduction

The Case for Exploring Race with Our Children

What is it like to be multiracial? How does it feel?

AS A YOUNG woman, I remember being asked the question "How does it feel to be **multiracial**? It must be so cool!" Staring blankly at the person who asked me this question, who indeed was eager and excited to learn more, I felt "othered" and that I didn't belong within the social gathering of teens I had been invited to, when I just wanted to fit in. Looking back at my youth, I recall feeling confusion when I would go to friends' houses and their caregivers and housekeepers were Filipina—like my own mother, who was a nurse—so I would just not bring up that part of myself and would focus attention on the South Asian part of my identity, because I unconsciously tied being Filipina to someone who was in the role of a servant, and felt shame about that. This is painful to admit— especially given my pride in **Filipinx** identity now—but is the cold, hard truth. At the same time, in elementary school, I was called "brownie" or made fun of because I "smelled of curry" by White classmates who thought it was funny or powerful to denounce my visible Brown and Pakistani heritage. So, perhaps being celebrated for being multiracial in my teenage years was a step up?

My years in university were exploratory and formative and I discovered the idea of having more than one identity due to a class on English literature taught by a professor named Dr. Gabriele Helms who threw out the "traditional" syllabus and brought forth a contemporary one on immigrant stories. Through that class, we had the opportunity to explore a range of cultural identities in multicultural Canadian society by a variety of authors, including M. G. Vassanji, who wrote the book *No New Land*.[1] This was one of the books in this class that exposed me to ideas of diaspora and hybridity that would later change the course of my entire life. I recall going to the bookstacks at my university and staring at the shelves in wonder—having discovered an entire section in the library on the very topic of multiplicity and belonging to more than one space, due to a paper I had to write for this English literature class. My eyes were wide open. *There could be more than one way to be; there could be multiple identities at the same time.* My mind was blown. Books for me were the gateway to this new understanding. It is coming full circle that I am writing one now, in order to help support that wonder, discovery, and exploration in others.

It wasn't until I went to graduate school at the University of Hawai'i at Mānoa that a world opened up for me about truly honoring my multiracial heritage in an intentional way. I recall in my first week on campus when I went to a student services office and a clerk attending to me pleasantly complimented my name and asked about my ethnic background. "I am Filipina and Pakistani," I announced, expecting the frequent response of "Oh, that's interesting," "How unique!" or something of that nature. Instead, this woman warmly offered back, "Oh, I am Hawaiian, Japanese, English, Portuguese, and Puerto Rican." She had said this with such ease and a spirit of community and camaraderie, of unity in the multiplicity instead of difference. For the first time, I felt belonging and that it was natural to have many cultures as a part of my heritage. I was speechless, taking this in. Notice that she mentioned each of her ethnic identities, clearly and equally. It was a moment that I would remember vividly, as I later learned more about the cultural migration to the islands for plantation work, the punctuated history and treatment of Native Hawaiians, and how the identity of "local" and belonging as a *kamaʻāina* superseded any differences. One could have many identities acknowledged, and still be accepted as a person, as who they are—and be completely "normal"—at the same time. Of course, there were and still are societal stratifications and hierarchies there, clear evidence of **colorism, marginalization** of some groups over others, and problematic practices in organizations related to racial and cultural identities. The sharing of my story is not to paint an idyllic picture of the islands as a paradise of **racial equity;** it is to acknowledge my personal experience of what it is like to be in a space where being multiracial is seen, accepted, understood, and not categorized as different, exotic, or other.

I didn't know before moving there about how high a percentage of multiracial population there was in Honolulu and in Hawaiʻi overall and was drawn to explore this further. I focused my graduate work on identity development of **multiethnic** youth and communication patterns that framed their understanding of identity, including interviews of multiracial Native Hawaiians and others, which was later published. I got involved in activism related to Filipinx veterans and youth leadership development, and was involved in leadership at the East-West Center and explored global relations among North America, Asia, the Pacific Islands, and the rest of the world. At the close of my time living in Hawaiʻi, I got married and added to the statistic of one out of every two marriages on the islands being multiracial. Hawaiʻi was not a surreal utopia to me; it was a *real* experience of belonging as a multiracial person, connection to the *ʻāina,* my ancestors, and my community, and finally feeling a sense of being able to hold my head up with pride in my identity in a way that I had never done before. This feeling and experience are ultimately what I keep coming back to when I work as a **diversity, equity,** and **inclusion** facilitator and consultant. If only organizations, communities, schools, and families would create environments that could cultivate a sense of belonging that I felt in that time period, which was so impactful for me.

As a parent and as a teacher educator, I wish for that sense of belonging for our young and grown children. This journey of my own upbringing, the struggle and strife and dissonance, and the resolution as a fully embodied multiethnic individual, is part of my story and could be a part of others' stories. And others' stories could be completely different from mine, in their process of realizing or grappling with identity. They may have different experiences, positive and negative, or neutral, that lead to how they adopt a sense of self similar to or different from that of their family members or friends. All of these are possibilities that we can explore as we look at supporting multiracial children. Most important is to recognize that there is no one linear path for multiracial identity development, and to be expansive in our conceptions of identity formation and the experiences we or our children face.

> *Why acknowledge differences? Why can't we all*
> *love and accept and teach children equally?*
> *Why isn't that enough?*

I get asked quite frequently whether surfacing the idea of **race** with a child would emphasize differences rather than similarities and create more division than cohesion within a community, school, or family. I am often challenged by people who say that bringing up the idea of race is not appropriate for children, and that we should instead emphasize our similarities to achieve a sense of normalcy within and among our children. Is it shattering a sense of innocence in our children by talking about controversial issues such as race? Why isn't raising all children the same way—with love, care, tenderness, and an emphasis on their talents and overall growth—where we should focus our energies and attention? Is it even appropriate to bring up race and difference within schools or in family settings? Where will all this talk about race get us?

I recall teaching a workshop at a school where a couple of White parents who had adopted children of a different race questioned why we should look at race at all. I gave the example of a news story that had circulated about a young White boy in elementary school who had wanted to cut his hair like his Black friend—and then after he had done that, he proudly stated how he looked just like his friend. This story went viral and many people thought it was a cute, heartwarming account of how children are innocent, are "**color-blind**,"[2] and are therefore accepting of others, regardless of race. Although this example may initially leave us with a warm and fuzzy feeling, the detrimental effects of not talking about race can happen as children get older (or even when they are young) and are questioned by society, are oppressed, and are later unprepared to deal with it.

The danger in not talking about race is adeptly illustrated by the StoryCorps segment "Traffic Stop."[3] This segment won an Emmy for News & Documentary and is a poignant story of a Black child whose White mother attempted to raise him in a color-blind world. The tragedy that ensued was a violent beating and near death of this young Black man after a traffic stop by Denver police. The story is incredibly moving because in StoryCorps format, it is an audio-recorded conversation between the young man and his mother, and she admits trying to just treat him like a person and with love. One can hear the emotions and pain in both of their voices in realizing that despite positive intentions, this approach was not enough. The brutal awakening that this family experienced comes as a warning and message to all of us.

Another example comes from a community gathering I was at recently where a young teen who identified as multiracial with one Black and one White parent shared openly about how he had trouble fitting in completely with either side of his family, and was teased to the point where his neighbors, who were also teens, tried to hang him with a noose as a game.

These examples are not historical from a time we consider yesteryear and no longer relevant. No, these instances took place recently and are moments that multiracial individuals can experience in varying degrees at any point in their lives. How do we ready our children for the possibility of any of these experiences happening?

We therefore must absolutely acknowledge race, racial differences, and the context of the society we live in—in order to best prepare our children to face potential circumstances, and also to cultivate positive self-worth and a larger awareness of contextual factors at play. The work is to become aware of these circumstances, factors, and perceptions as parents and educators, even when we may not be exposed to them ourselves.

Moving beyond Color-Blindness

"I see no difference. I treat everyone the same."

Exploring this conception of awareness of a child's identity as both ourselves as adults and themselves as children can also lead us to think about how we can be better advocates and **allies** in their lives. Essential to preparing to take that action is an examination of our own conceptions of how we approach race, especially with multiracial children who—due to their multiplicity—may be of a different ethnic heritage than us. It is very likely that the multiracial child may have a different identity than we do as parents, caregivers, or educators in their lives. Or even if they are of the same racial composition as we are, they may identify differently, due to their physical appearance, experiences with others, or society's reinforcement of their identity, among other factors. How do we best prepare to deal with the plethora of possibilities?

As in the case mentioned previously captured by StoryCorps, Alex Landau and his mother Patsy Hathaway share dialogue that delves deeper into the complexities of raising a child who phenotypically looks different from their parent. Alex's mother says, "I thought that love would conquer all and skin color really didn't matter. I had to learn the hard way, when they almost killed you."

In terms of multiracial identity, speaking to race is a very important aspect of caregiving and education. As a Japanese and White individual describes a wish, "For my monoracial parents to have had open and honest conversations with me about race! Growing up in the US, my parents never talked about race with me and in retrospect, I felt very ill-prepared as someone who was multiracial to enter a racialized world upon leaving home to enter college."

The well-intentioned thinking of ignoring racial differences within the classroom or the family home is something that can naturally be what we turn to as educators and parents. Our moral compass and societal upbringing may have reinforced the idea that being "color-blind" and "treating all children the same" are ways of being fair, being consistent, and also honoring the child for who they are, not what they look like. During my practicum in training to become a certified schoolteacher, I distinctly remember my assigned mentor teacher telling me, "I don't see differences in the classroom." Although this may seem appropriate to pass onto others or adopt in one's own philosophy of education, the reality is that by ignoring differences in children, we are erasing the very complexity and nuances that each child brings to the table. Not only does that undermine a healthy sense of unique identity within them, but it leaves them completely unprepared for the inevitable responses in society by other individuals, including family members or colleagues, who may notice and comment or act on the differences they see. There also are systemic processes within society overall and **implicit bias** within organizations that may impact our children due to their race. In my organizational consulting work with corporations, nonprofits, and higher-education institutions, I have seen this play out even at the adult level. This shows how dialogue and purposeful guidance in a child's formative years can help prepare them for future experiences. These examples demonstrate how it is important to acknowledge racial and cultural differences while at the same time raising and nurturing children overall in their development as human beings.

Child Development and Readiness

Are children ready to talk about race?

We may feel that young children are not at the age to acknowledge racial differences and that discussions about race are not relevant or appropriate in early childhood. The truth is that children are indeed aware of race, starting from a very young age. A powerful image illustrating research around this fact was created by the Children's Community School,[4] based in part on information and ideas from Jillian Adler at First Up, Lori Riddick at Raising Race Conscious Children, and kiran nigam at AORTA.

As depicted in this image from the Children's Community School, children start to notice differences about race from infancy. Numerous studies have shown how children recognize racial differences and even express preferences, at an early age.

Figure 1. "They're Not Too Young to Talk about Race," Children's Community School

As the research and visual depiction show, children's awareness of race begins very early on. In fact, the early years of a child's development are a key foundational time to instill a holistic picture of identity, individual and group relationships, a fulfilling experience of being multiracial, and belonging in a society that is accepting and celebrating of racial difference. Given this knowledge, as educators and parents, what are we doing to scaffold a healthy sense of positive self-identity within multiracial children? How are we creating supportive environments within the classroom, home, or community to address the unique needs of multiracial children specifically?

Addressing race in the classroom or home can be challenging in itself, and adding the layer of multiracial identity can be something that we can often overlook or may feel unprepared to deal with.

Adult Development and Readiness

Truthfully, what may be at the heart of the matter is: are *we* as adults ready to talk about race? As we can see in the news and even in our own experiences with others, race is not something that is easily described, understood, or dealt with in a single way. We may be comfortable talking about race, but what about those around us who are not? There are myriad factors that can hinder healthy conversations about race, or that can advance understanding toward actions that benefit all—including our own readiness. Added to this is the presence of **inequity, systemic oppression,** implicit bias, power and **privilege** dynamics, and societal injustice regarding race that make for a potentially volatile and oppositional environment that can prevent us from being able to fully engage without doubt, discomfort, or uncertainty. We may feel that we are not equipped to begin the dialogue, or perhaps we have had experiences where the dialogue has gone in unintended or undesired directions, reinforcing our hesitation to approach it at all. Or we could be fully aware of the aforementioned factors and are looking for more effective and creative ways to foster conversation and action.

Ultimately, you are reading this book to learn more, which is a major first step. An important part of this process is centering our children as the reason for embarking on this journey of exploration and understanding, honoring that it may be fraught with challenge and the need for healing, which requires acknowledging pain and discomfort, and also recognizing that we need to create space for development and awareness in *ourselves*. With this gentle awareness and intention to embrace this process as it unfolds uniquely for each of us, we can take steps toward cultivating a better experience at home and in school for multiracial children. We must also acknowledge that this is inherently messy work. There is no perfect way to talk about race. It is definitely a journey, and the effort is a work in progress.

Approach of This Book

The purpose of this book is to help develop a deeper understanding of race in relationship to multiracial identity, to provide an overview of key issues and current topics that are resonant in raising multiracial children, and to offer approaches and strategies that can be implemented in the classroom or at home.

Chapter 1 begins with a foundational understanding of race, an overview of terminology, and how race is conceived and categorized historically and now. In chapter 2, we will move into a reflection of adult **intercultural** development and Racial Dialogue Readiness, through a summary of selected key models that help us understand our approaches and readiness in our nurturing of children regarding aspects of race and identity, accompanied by recommended strategies. In chapter 3, we examine identity fluidity and racial rigidity, and how one develops **resilience** in navigating a multiracial identity in a racialized world. We will then explore factors affecting identity choice and assignment in chapter 4, including societal contextual factors, and how we conceive of and react to these factors can in turn shape a child's multiracial identity. Chapter 5 highlights common and contemporary issues facing multiracial children, including an explanation of **phenotype, microaggressions,** and **intersectionality.** Chapter 6 outlines developmental benchmarks for learning outcomes with children, and age-appropriate activities and strategies to cultivate multiracial identity development and an awareness of race. Chapter 7 calls out critical aspects of the college experience and beginning a career, and how entry into each of these realms presents its own specific areas of attention for multiracial individuals. Chapter 8 provides commentary and insight into the call for advocacy and action that can be taken in our roles as parents and educators, as well as the need for community-building. Lastly, chapter 9 captures a selection of recommended resources for use at home and in the classroom to initiate discussion and enhance learning about multiracial identity. The book ends with reference material in the form of appendices that offer a glossary of key terms, social justice educational standards, and additional teaching activities that can be useful for the reader to explore further and revisit at different stages in a child's life.

It was very important in the creation of this book that there be an exploration of conceptual understanding about this topic coupled with practical activities that can be utilized by education professionals, caregivers, and parents. As a parent, educator, and diversity, equity, and inclusion consultant, I approach this work as a bringing together of foundational knowledge and research that is instrumental to understanding multiracial identity, as well as best practices that have proved effective at home and in the classroom. Also, as an adult of multiethnic heritage and someone who has been an advocate and mentor in multiracial communities for many years, I will offer my reflections and perceptions throughout the book that may help peel away layers of fogginess around this topic to provide clarity, due to my intimate experience with these issues.

My intention is to support learning by the reader by capturing key elements from academic research, identity development theory, current events, classroom-based strategies, and real experiences from families and schools in order to offer a picture of understanding that can be found elsewhere, but in a vast array of resources. I have specifically included powerful quotes and examples from multiracial individuals and parents of multiracial children sharing firsthand experiences and situations they have faced. Although some details may have been slightly altered to protect the identity of the individuals, these examples are all based on true stories and demonstrate the circumstances in which multiracial identity is perceived and navigated. By bringing together these elements cohesively in this form, along with my own expertise and commentary, I hope that this book will accelerate an understanding of this topic in order to lead to awareness, reflection, conversation, and action toward supporting multiracial children.

1

Who Are Multiracial Individuals?

WHERE DO WE BEGIN? Let's start with who we are talking about.

Who are multiracial people? Multiracial people are people whose identity is composed of more than one race. According to the United States Census Bureau's 2010 census,[1] multiracial people constitute almost 3% of the entire US population, or approximately 9 million people. An increase in the multiracial population of 32% from the previous census in comparison with an increase of 9% in the single-race population means that multiracial individuals are one of the fastest growing groups in the United States.

Terminology

As we begin this dialogue, an important aspect to consider is: how are we describing multiracial identity? What is the right term to use? Multiracial? Mixed race? Half-something?? What should our children call themselves? Terminology is extremely important in living out any racial identity, as it indicates how people see themselves.

Also, preference for a certain term can vary from person to person. Let's go over some key terms related to race and multiracial identity.

Race: a social construct that has been proved to have no biological basis, and is largely conceived as group membership based on common physical characteristics.

Ethnicity: group membership based on a common cultural heritage.

Nationality: relating to the country where a person was born and/or holds citizenship.

Culture: the customary beliefs, social forms, and material traits of a racial, religious, or social group.

Multiracial: identity of two or more races.

Biracial: identity of two races.

Mixed race: identity referring to the mixing of two or more races. Someone may refer to themselves as "mixed" as a shorthand for mixed race. Although generally seen as positive, some people take offense to the term "mixed" because they feel it connotes that a person is "mixed-up." Many people use this term interchangeably with multiracial.

Multiethnic: identity of two or more ethnicities.

More terms and a discussion related to multiracial identity terminology can be found at the end of this chapter, as well as within the glossary in Appendix A. And now you may be wondering: how has history impacted the race categories we have today?

The United States Census

To understand more about race, we must take a close look at the census, the official count and demographic survey of the population within a given region. A historical timeline of the United

States Census[2] highlights how individuals didn't even have racial categories that adequately described people in the United States until very recently. The first categorizations were "free white males, free white females," "slaves," and "all other free persons," found in the 1790 census. Later, there came a category of "free colored males and females" in 1820. Over time, these categories came to include the terms "**Mulatto**" or "Mulatto slaves" in 1850 to acknowledge the race mixing that had been occurring, as well as the term "Black" in the same year. The term "Indian" was added in 1860—finally acknowledging the Native peoples who were already on the land that was inhabited by White colonial settlers, yet were not separately counted previously. There were also terms such as "**Quadroon**" and "**Octoroon**" added in 1890, further breaking down the Black/White biracial identity into fractions. These furthered the rules of hypodescent, also known as the "one-drop rule," which ensured that people with any bit of Black heritage would be considered Black, to preserve the power of and land ownership by White individuals. In 1900, "Mulatto" and other racial-mixing terms were removed, leaving people to choose between "White" or "Black (Negro or of Negro descent)." "Mulatto" came back in 1910 and 1920, and then was removed again in 1930, the same year the term "Black" changed to "Negro."

In parallel, there was the addition of Asian racial categories: first "Chinese" in 1870, then "Japanese" was added in 1890, and "Filipino," "Korean," and "Hindu" were added in 1920. In 1930, "Mexicans" were counted as a separate race for the first time. The year 1960 was paramount, when the terms "Aleut," "Eskimo," and "American Indian" were listed on the census, along with the addition of "Hawaiian" and "Part Hawaiian," and individuals were finally able to choose their own race—rather than a census taker (enumerator) filling it out for them—and potentially assigning their race. From 1970 on, there was finally the addition of "Central or South American," "Mexican," "Puerto Rican," "Cuban," and "Other

Spanish" as categories—but these were not considered races. Also the term "Other" was a racial category that could be chosen, and the category "Negro" expanded to "Negro, or Black." From 1980 onward, the term "Asian Indian" was added, along with "Vietnamese," "Samoan," and "Guamanian," although Asians and Pacific Islanders were categorized together in 1990, along with the "Other Asian or Pacific Islander" label. The year 2000 was a major milestone year in that individuals were finally able to choose more than one race with the new instructions to "Mark one or more races." That same year, the term "African American" was added to the category "Black, or Negro," and Native Hawaiian and Pacific Islanders were counted in a separate category from Asians.[3] The prompt "Is this person Spanish/Hispanic/Latino?" still remains a separate question from the race question, and this confuses many individuals, as they have to answer both this ethnic heritage question and the race question, even though people may feel that this is a race.

Who designs these questions? In its current form, the US Census Bureau "collects information on race following the guidance of the US Office of Management and Budget's (OMB) 1997 Revisions to the Standards for the Classification of Federal Data on Race and Ethnicity.[4] These federal standards mandate that race and Hispanic origin (ethnicity) are separate and distinct concepts and that, when collecting these data via self-identification, two different questions must be used." It's important to note that this distinction between race and ethnicity doesn't allow someone who is multiracial of Spanish/Hispanic/Latino heritage to be properly identified in the count of more than one race unless they select two or more different races (e.g., Black, White, and Hispanic), since choosing this ethnic identity plus a single race (e.g., White and Hispanic) does not qualify a person as multiracial. Also, you may notice that many state and local forms are modeled after the guidelines set out by the OMB.

With the new data gathered with the change in the ability to check more than one race, we are able to get a sense of the multiracial population in the country, and really grasp the presence of those who identify with more than one race. I recall the first time we as a family filled out the US Census form that had "Mark one or more races." I was many months pregnant. We were behind on our to-do list, and the mail among other tasks had piled up—those of you who are pregnant or who have children can relate!—so we had not filled out the form and mailed it in. Finally, a US Census Bureau representative came to the door and reminded us to complete the form. I answered the door thinking, Wow, how will we fill this out for our little one? My husband joked with me that he "didn't want to fill this thing out wrong" given all the work I was doing with the multiracial community, how conscious I was about identity, and the fact that we were both multiethnic and he was multiracial. I had to study the questions and really think about how to answer them. Such are the challenges of being multiethnic or multiracial and filling out the census form—it really gives us pause and makes us think about who we want to define ourselves as.

Have you ever been confused or had questions about where you fit into the census racial categories? If so, that is understandable! Let's go over them. For the 2010 US Census, the US Census Bureau[5] defines "White" as a person having origins in any of the original peoples of Europe, the Middle East, or North Africa. "Black or African American" refers to a person having origins in any of the Black racial groups of Africa. "American Indian or Alaska Native" refers to a person having origins in any of the original peoples of North and South America, including Central America, and who "maintains a tribal affiliation or community attachment." The term "Asian" refers to a person having origins in any of the original peoples of the Far East, Southeast Asia, or the Indian subcontinent. "Native Hawaiian or Other Pacific Islander" refers to a person having origins in any of the original peoples of Hawai'i, Guam, Samoa, or other Pacific Islands. "Some Other Race" includes all responses not included in the aforementioned categories. The category "Hispanic or Latino" is considered an ethnic group, indicating a person's heritage, nationality group, lineage, or country of birth. "Hispanic or Latino" refers to a person of Cuban, Mexican, Puerto Rican, South or Central American, or other Spanish-speaking culture, regardless of race. So, on the census, you would choose one or more of the races, and indicate if you are either "Hispanic or Latino" or not. Although the US Census Bureau sees Hispanic origin as a separate concept from race, many people self-reported that as race on the form anyway, writing it in the category of "Some Other Race."

According to the 2000 US Census,[6] 6.8 million people equaling 2.4% of the total US population self-reported as belonging to more than one race. Of these, 42% of individuals who checked more than one race were under the age of eighteen, which contrasts with 25% of individuals who checked a single race who were under the age of eighteen. We should note that in the 2000 census, the American Indian and Alaska Native (AIAN) population and the Native Hawaiian and Other Pacific Islanders (NHOPI) population represented the highest percentage of individuals reporting more than one race, among the races. This translates into 39.9% of the AIAN population, or 1.6 million American Indian and Alaska Native individuals, identifying as more than one race; and 54.4% of NHOPI people, or 476,000 Native Hawaiian and Other Pacific Islanders individuals, reporting more than one race.

This overall number of multiracial individuals grew to 2.9% of the population, or a population of 9 million, as reported by the 2010 US Census. There are some other notable statistics about the multiracial population. The largest combination within this group is "White" and "Some Other Race" numbering 2.2 million or 32% of the multiracial population, followed by "White" and "American Indian or Alaska Native" representing 1.1 million individuals at about 16% of the multiracial population. Ninety-two percent of people who reported multiple races provided exactly two races on the 2010 US Census. White and Black were the largest specific multiple-race combination. Also, an additional 8% of the two or more races population reported three races, and less than 1% reported four or more races.[7]

Nearly 70% of the multiracial population at the time of the 2010 census were under the age of thirty-five. As Nicholas Jones, then-chief of the US Census Bureau's Racial Statistics Branch, stated, "Overall, the total US population increased by 9.7 percent since 2000, however, many multiple-race groups increased by 50 percent or more."[8] If we look at the population of multiracial children under the age of eighteen specifically, this group has increased by almost 50% to 4.2 million, making it the fastest growing youth group in the country.[9]

Of the individuals who marked more than one race in the 2010 US Census, 83% of those individuals reported White as part of their racial heritage. The largest combinations of individuals marking two or more races overall were Black and White (20.4%), White and Some Other Race (19.3%), Asian and White (18%), and American Indian or Alaska Native and White (15.9%).

Those with "multiple-minority race" responses on the 2010 US Census (i.e., individuals who marked more than one race, not including the White race) totaled 1.5 million people. Of the multiple-minority race data, most respondents were Black and Some Other Race (20.7%), American Indian or Alaska Native and Black (17.7%), all other multiple-minority race combinations (15.5%), and Asian and Some Other Race (15.4%). The fastest growing groups who checked more than one race showing change from 2000 to 2010 include Black and Asian (73.8% increase), Native Hawaiian or Other Pacific Islander and Black (68.4% increase), Native Hawaiian or Other Pacific Islander and Some Other Race (68.0% increase), American Indian or Alaska Native and Native Hawaiian or Other Pacific Islander (50.6% increase), and American Indian or Alaska Native and Black (47.6% increase).[10]

According to the US Census Bureau's 2017 American Community Survey population estimate,[11] there is an estimate of approximately 10.1 million people who would check more than one race. Since the American Community Survey is a population profile that serves as a robust estimate, the percentages of each racial category are expected to remain the same within the 2020 US Census.

In terms of **interracial** unions in the United States, the percentage of married-couple households that are interracial or interethnic grew from 7.4% in 2000 to 10.2% in 2010. The largest group of interracial/interethnic married-couple combinations was of non-Hispanic Whites married to Hispanics, which increased in 43% of the counties across the United States.[12] The largest growth was seen in Hawai'i, Oklahoma, and Washington, DC, with an increase in interracial couples of over 4% for each region. An important historical event to note is the federal ruling of *Loving v. Virginia* on June 12, 1967,[13] which deemed interracial unions legal, when interracial marriage was previously banned in many states. It is also worth noting that although this was a federal ruling, some states like Alabama did not enact the law until as late as the year 2000. One can see how historical events can influence the rise of interracial relationships and the birth of multiracial children.

Statistics Canada

The same growing trends can be seen in the population of Canada from the most recent Statistics Canada data from 2016. According to Statistics Canada,[14] over 14.1 million of the total Canadian population of more than 35.1 million people listed themselves as having multiple ethnic origins. But one should note that this can include ethnicities from the same racial grouping. Also, those who listed themselves as "multiple visible minorities," which "includes persons who gave more than one visible minority group by checking two or more mark-in responses, e.g., 'Black' and 'South Asian,'" composed 0.7% of the population, or approximately 232,000 individuals. Of Canadians with Aboriginal ancestry, nearly 4%, or 1.4 million individuals, are of Aboriginal and non-Aboriginal ancestry. Another interesting statistic is that of generational shift in ethnic origin. The longer an immigrant group is settled in Canada, the more likely it is that it will reflect multiple ethnicities. This can be seen in the data reported that shows 17.8% of first-generation Canadians report multiple ethnicities, whereas the second generation reports 45.3% and third-generation groups report 49.3% multiple ethnicities within an ethnic group.

Interethnic unions have been on the rise in Canada for nearly the past three decades. According to the 2011 National Household Survey, more than 360,000 couples, or 4.6% of all married and common-law couples, in Canada were in mixed unions. In the area where I grew up as a youth, 9.6% of Vancouver-area couples are made up of partners from different ethnic backgrounds, which is higher per capita than any other Canadian city.[15]

As we can see from this data from both the United States and Canada, a focus on multiracial and multiethnic populations is essential, as they make up some of the largest growing segments of our population today and will likely increase with the projections about the multiracial and multiethnic populations, as well as the increase in interracial unions.[16]

More from the Pew Research Center

What's interesting when we look at this further is how these numbers could likely be underestimating the actual multiracial population that exists in the United States. According to the Pew Research Center, the number of multiracial individuals is likely to be closer to 6.9% of the entire US population, rather than 2.9%. Why is this? The reason is that some people are mixed race even if they don't claim it. Pew's own comprehensive study of multiracial individuals demonstrated that many individuals claim a single-race heritage, even though they may have a parent or grandparent who is a different race. This means that many individuals are mixed race but may fill out the census acknowledging only one of their races.

So what is going on here? Why aren't people listing their true racial backgrounds? We can't answer that question without taking a deeper look at the history of the country, including government policies that marginalized people due to race, as well as societal norms that forced people to choose one race or be perceived as one race and be marginalized. It also could be due to social factors and an affinity with or preference for one race over another, not to mention what individuals are taught about race by family members or other valued people in their lives. There is so much at play here.

Following patterns of the US Census gives us clues as to how people from different races were treated, and also how Black, **Indigenous,** and other **People of Color** (**BIPOC**) as well as multiracial people were acknowledged or not recognized over time. It also points to a deeper story of systemic oppression, marginalization, legal exclusion, and other atrocities committed in the name of the law and economic progress that punctuate our history. In this narrative, we cannot forget the activism by advocates within multiracial organizations convened by the Association of MultiEthnic Americans (AMEA) to even have the ability to be recognized and counted, and these efforts culminating in the 2000 landmark change to the census that finally allowed individuals to be able to check more than one race on the form. Did you know that at the time of this advocacy, civil rights groups such as the National Association for the Advancement of Colored People (NAACP),[17] the Mexican American Legal Defense and Educational Fund (MALDEF), and the National Coalition for an Accurate Count of Asian Pacific Americans initially were "vehemently opposed" to the possibility of adding a multiracial category or other distinction for multiracial individuals?[18] There was fear that the addition of this option would lessen the count of other already underrepresented groups, thereby compromising potential funding in the form of federal aid that was tied to representation. These are facts we cannot ignore and must speak about. This history is what brought us here today, in this polarized society that emphasizes a racialized existence. These historical events and the impacts of racial categorization and racial hierarchies pit groups against one another. Some of those mindsets still exist today and are passed onto our children—as they learn to choose one side of their identity over another, or are pressed to do this, to prove loyalty to a cause or belonging within a group. Or are judged by how they behave, look, or sound. This is the world in which our children live. What can we do to support our children's multiracial identity development in an authentic and positive way, given this context?

Multiracial Descriptors

Now that we have a historical and current background on racial categories and have been introduced to some terminology, let's explore some other descriptors related to multiracial identity:

Transracial adoptee: identity of being adopted by a family of a different race than the adoptee. A child can be multiracial as well as a transracial adoptee.

Hapa: being of mixed ethnic heritage (the term originated in Hawaiʻi and is from the Hawaiian language, meaning "part"). In some locales, it is often used to indicate mixed Asian heritage, and is both a celebrated and contested term.

Third culture kids (TCKs): children raised in a culture other than their parents' culture or passport country for a significant part of their early development. A child can be a TCK and be multiracial at the same time.

The following are some terms that have had negative connotations in the past that are sometimes used casually, or are intentionally used as a form of empowerment over a derogatory term: mulatto, half-breed, Hafu (in Japan).

A combination of racial or ethnic terms can be used to uniquely identify a person's mixed racial heritage. Examples include "Blaxican," "Mexipino," "Chindian," and "Whasian." These terms are positive and are often used to fondly refer to one's heritage, usually within personal relationships.

What about Those Fractions?

Saying a person is "half-Brazilian and half-Japanese" or is a "quarter Black" is commonly heard. However, this can be viewed as cutting a child into parts, or identifying one's affinity to a racial heritage by the racial percentage or blood quantum count. Given the punctuated historical context we live in, this can be problematic. Instead, a way to invite a child to honor all aspects of their racial heritage equally would be to say that they are "Native American and Lebanese." That way there is a sense of fullness and togetherness, rather than a pulling apart, or "measuring" from one's own viewpoint, or by others.

As one responded who is Filipino and White shares, "I am training myself not to call myself half anymore. Half Filipino or half white. I'm trying to use the language of both or two because it makes me feel like I have a gift instead of a deficiency. It would have been helpful if my family growing up described me as both instead of half/half. I wanted to be valued as a whole person."

It is important to reiterate this with your children, so they can appreciate a full acceptance of both of their cultures. A person identifying as Mexican, Spanish, Native Hawaiian, and British shares, "After constant years of actually learning my cultures and what it means to me, I've learned that I'm not 50% of one or 20% of another, but I am 100% each of my ethnic backgrounds."

REFLECTION

Notice what you think about your child's racial identity and the words used to describe your child. Compare this with what your child may prefer as a self-identifying term. What do you find?

What if the child is not someone you know personally? How should you refer to them?

It is important to have a clear understanding of how the child identifies, and this may involve a conversation with the child's parents, as well as the child. Do not make assumptions about a child's racial or ethnic identity.

A multiracial child's identity can be changing and different from the identity of siblings or what their parents wish for them. We will be exploring the complexity of the development of multiracial identity throughout this book.

Through opening up the dialogue and awareness of the history and terminology about multiracial people, parents, caregivers, and educators can start to craft a process where racial identity is something that is cultivated in a deeper and meaningful way.

2

Adult Intercultural Development and Racial Dialogue Readiness

Race has object permanence. It is still there, no matter how hard we try to look away.

—FARZANA NAYANI

IN WORKING WITH a multitude of groups, families, and individuals across many different cities and educational institutions, I have noticed one thing that is a common factor in the ability to advance a conversation about race: readiness.

By and large, readiness is probably one of the most critical factors not only for having a conversation about race, but also for implementing both short-term and long-term actions to nurture personal growth and racial identity development in multiracial and transracially adopted individuals.

Familiarity and Discomfort

There is a real hesitation and discomfort in bringing up the topic of race with regards to children. Many teachers and parents are extremely uncomfortable in doing so, sharing reasons of feeling unprepared or inadequate in being able to talk about race with children. They also state that they don't want to cause negative impact by raising a topic that doesn't seem to be an issue up to that point. This may be you, and if it is—know that you are not alone.

Before I begin a workshop on talking about race and **culture,** I often ask individuals in the session—educators, parents, administrators—what their fears may be. One very common fear is of offending another person. This in itself shows beautiful intentions and a deep care and protection for the children they are raising and teaching. However, this intention may have a grave impact in later years.

The problem with the lack of dialogue about race due to the fear of offending another person is that children will be wholly unprepared to deal with situations having to do with race if they have not talked about it with a trusted adult. The results of this lack of preparedness can lead to experiences from surprise to emotional harm, lack of confidence, and perhaps even life-threatening situations where a child's safety is at risk. The benefits of talking about race largely outweigh the discomfort that can arise in bringing it up with a child. Additionally, the risks of *not* talking about race are far too high, especially in this current climate where racial identification can be the cause of hatred that can lead to violence or harm.

Part of the discomfort that adults feel comes from the absence of reflection on the part of the individual to explore and face the positionality of their own identities within the larger context of society. What may arise from this reflection is that there could be marginalization that an adult finds is traumatic to relive. Or there could be sorrow and guilt that arise from the awareness that an adult's racial identity leads to unearned privilege, which is incredibly painful and alarming. The hurt and suffering that come from the awareness of inequity due to race may cause a parent or educator to want to actively avoid the topic altogether.

The inherent risk of feeling this way, coupled with media and societal conceptions of race that are volatile and polarizing, can make one unwilling to bring up the topic. Instead, the default approach may be to minimize the situation by taking the color-blind position that "all children should be treated equally" in an attempt to make the problem go away. With this, people feel all bases are covered. After all, teaching children citizenship and values of respect and being good people should be enough for a family or classroom. But is this really so? Does this truly prepare children for instances of sudden self-awareness that they are different? Or for instances of intentional or unintentional othering by the child's friend who notices that their facial or other physical features don't match others around them? The absence of dialogue may cause shock within children when they are faced with these or other challenging settings.

An additional risk is that adults, upon further reflection, may have the overwhelming experience of discovering that inequity is rampant in many facets of their lives, but don't feel equipped to do anything about it. Adults may not know where to start the conversation about racial identity, and also multiracial identity. All of these reasons can prevent adults from going down the path of facing this at all. The thought is: if we don't look at it, it won't come up in our lives. A stark example of this comes from an individual who identifies as Japanese and White. They share, "Realizing at a young age that my parents, neither of whom are mixed race, didn't understand the situations in which I felt subjected to my multiracial background was difficult. For example, when I was visiting Japan as a young child, strangers would often look at me on trains. I didn't like this attention, and when I brought it up to my Japanese mom, she always brushed it off with a mere 'Just don't think about it.' This made me think about it all the more, since the root issue was never addressed. I wish she would have at least acknowledged and validated how I felt self-conscious and uncomfortable." The reality of race exists, even though we wish to ignore it.

Just as we teach young children the idea of **object permanence** through the game of peekaboo, the exercise of looking at race makes it something recognizable and more understandable with time. In the same way that the face behind our hands does not go away when we play peekaboo, the race of our children also has object permanence—no matter how hard we try to look away. Color-blindness in a society that is far from color-blind does not work.

Furthering this analogy, adults can practice "looking at race" through conversation, consuming information about how to address issues, continued dialogue, and reflection, and through repeated contact with instances where they can practice learned strategies. Through this process, they will become used to the idea that race is indeed a factor in children's lives; inequity exists; and it is important to learn strategies for how to be equipped to deal with this reality. After these aspects of understanding are internalized, an adult can further explore best practices about how to cultivate a positive and healthy identity for children who are multiracial.

One important note related to an inequity of experiences is that the ability to "look away" from race is largely tied to privilege. This is usually done by parents and educators who are themselves posi-tioned as part of the dominant race in their society or institution, or who have mitigating characteristics such as economic and social class that buffer the experience of race. Also, children who "pass" or are "read" as the dominant culture (i.e., physically look like the dominant culture, even though their racial makeup may consist of more than that culture) can experience the resulting privilege of being able to fit in. There are blindspots caused by these mitigating characteristics that can leave a gaping hole in not understanding the need to talk about race. After all, if children work hard and are provided with access to and opportunities for education and other activities, they should be able to move toward success, right? The issue with this thinking is that we don't live in a vacuum, and there will be—guaranteed—a moment in the future when a shocking experience of a child will send this reality into question. Will they be prepared to deal with it, then?

In contrast, those adults and children who possess or represent marginalized or underprivileged identities within their neighborhood or school will have a completely different experience. Instead of being able to look away from race, the opposite experience may occur, where adults and children *can't* look away. They will likely be faced with racially driven experiences and issues on a regular basis.

A study of six thousand parents, conducted by Sesame Workshop and NORC at the University of Chicago, published by NPR confirms this.[1] When families were asked if they talk about differences in social identities, research showed that more parents of color (61% of Black parents, 56% of Asian parents, and 51% of Hispanic parents) talked to their children about race and ethnicity than did White parents (25%). The survey also showed that "many of the parents who are talking not just about race/ethnicity but also gender, class and religion are doing so because their children are hearing negative comments about their own identities." Parents from POC groups who had heard feedback about their own identity throughout their lives were more likely to talk to their children about race and ethnicity. As we can see, the experience of being a marginalized person can prompt the conversation about race and ethnicity in families. POC parents and educators may be more ready than White counterparts because they have had to experience negative encounters themselves. What does that mean for families with a White parent, or for the many educational institutions that have predominantly White faculty?

One educator I met who is a Black mother of a biracial child and who works with a mostly White teaching staff commented on how she grew up having to talk about it in her living room on a regular basis with her family, whereas her White colleagues and partner would not be able to completely understand what that is like. She described how painful it was to hear her five-year-old son declare that he wished that he looked more "vanilla" than "chocolate." This real difference in the lived experience of racial identity can be present among teaching staff or within couples where different racial backgrounds of adults are present. As a result, there may be a wide range of comfort and readiness, within families or school environments, in talking about or dealing with racial situations. This shows how each of us may have different needs in the process of this exploration.

Each person's experiences and needs require careful reflection and may call for different resources in terms of support and dialogue to deepen understanding and move forward. An important step is determining where we are in that journey.

Models to Explore: Are Adults Ready to Have Dialogue?

There are various models that describe one's approach to differences and that capture the stages of readiness that a person can feel about exploring race and culture. These frameworks can be helpful in understanding and determining your own capacity and approach when talking about race. Although they are not billed as "readiness" models per se, I've listed them here in this way as strong indicators of our openness to approaching dialogue and exploration about race.

The approach shared in this chapter supports reflection on and assessment of one's own comfort and readiness to talk about cultural and racial differences. The two models shared here are based on the Intercultural Development Continuum (IDC) and the Teaching Tolerance program guide. We also explore the Racial Dialogue

Readiness (RDR) self-reflective questionnaire and the Conscious Cultivation of Identity (CCI) model, which I have developed, and which also serve as a strategy. Using these tools may offer a helpful jumping-off point to consider your own approach in talking about race with children, as well as potential growth areas, blindspots, or gaps that need to be addressed in order to help foster a positive sense of identity for multiracial children.

Intercultural Development Continuum (IDC)

One well-known model from the intercultural field is the Intercultural Development Continuum (IDC) and its counterpart, the cross-culturally validated assessment tool, the Intercultural Development Inventory (IDI).[2] The IDC is adapted from the Developmental Model of Intercultural Sensitivity (DMIS) originally proposed by Milton Bennett.[3] Based on the IDC, the Intercultural Development Inventory is a tool used within organizations and educational institutions that charts individuals' mindsets toward cultural difference and commonality. More detailed information on this model and tool can be found at https://idiinventory.com.

The orientations are Denial, Polarization, Minimization, Acceptance, and Adaptation.

> **Denial.** The **Denial** orientation displays a disinterest in other cultures and an active avoidance of cultural differences. Individuals who have this orientation may see differences, but may not attribute them as "cultural." This orientation can be caused by limited experience with cultural groups and can lead to individuals operating with broadly held **stereotypes** and generalizations about others, as well as keeping a distance from other cultural groups.

> **Polarization.** The **Polarization** mindset views cultural differences in the framework of "us versus them." A **Defense** orientation is characterized by beliefs that "my culture is

better than others," and other cultures may seem to be a threat to a certain way of doing things, whereas a **Reversal** orientation perceives "other cultures are better than mine" and can cause an idealizing of other cultures while denigrating one's own group.

෨ **Minimization.** The **Minimization** orientation highlights the commonalities with other groups and also universal values and principles, but this can hide the acknowledgment of real differences among cultural groups. The drawback of this mindset is that the depth of cultural differences is masked or may be trivialized or romanticized.

෨ **Acceptance.** An **Acceptance** orientation recognizes differences among individuals as well as commonalities at the same time. There is a curiosity about and understanding of cultural differences as well as their complexity, but individuals may not be fully able to adapt to these differences appropriately. A person with an Acceptance orientation can acknowledge the differences of others but may have difficulty making decisions that impact a range of cultural groups.

෨ **Adaptation.** Those with an **Adaptation** orientation display cognitive and behavioral shifting that enables them to bridge diverse communities and navigate cultural differences. They exemplify strategies that are adaptive to the cultural context, and this range of frameworks helps them move through different cultural situations in a deeper and an involved way.

When reflecting upon the above, where do you fall in the continuum of intercultural development? What about your colleagues? Or family members? How do you think the mindsets—in yourself, and in others—exemplified by these orientations impact how you engage with others about race? How has privilege or systemic oppression or other experiences led you to the orientation you are in?

Intercultural Development Continuum

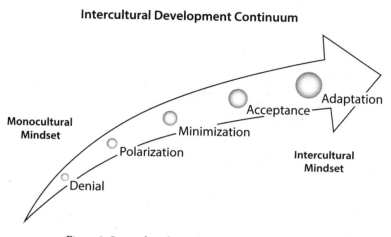

Figure 2. Intercultural Development Continuum (IDC)

This model demonstrates that there is a wide range in one's awareness of differences, and in one's capacity for navigating differences. This fundamental disposition among individuals is paramount in understanding one's approach to talking about cultural differences, including race. There are advantages and disadvantages to each IDC approach. How does this impact how we interact with children regarding race?

- **Denial.** If a parent or educator is in denial that cultural or racial differences are real or make a difference, the child may be brought up to believe this to be true.

- **Polarization.** If a parent or educator resents their own culture (polarizes) and tends to take on another culture more than their own culture, they may pass on that sentiment to their child, even though the child is a product of more than one culture. Or, if a parent or educator vehemently favors their own culture over another culture, this bias can also be passed onto the child.

- **Minimization** is what we have talked about already, where educators or parents may find themselves wanting to uphold a spirit of teaching or treating all children equally, thereby spending less time on or giving less attention to differences. Although this has positive intent, it can leave children—and adults—without the proper tools or awareness to face real issues when differences are pointed out to them at school or in other parts of their daily lives.

ð **Acceptance** of differences is a favorable step toward cultivating an environment where a child can recognize their multiracial identity in a holistic way, as differences are recognized and honored. There is an opportunity for growth in learning how to translate this understanding to behaviors and actions that honor the differences among different cultural groups.

ð The **Adaptation** orientation underscores the importance of taking action steps toward culturally sensitive and effective strategies for interacting with others.

While using this model, it is extremely important to supplement the conversation with analyzing how power and privilege dynamics affect an individual or group, and how moving toward a certain orientation may or may not be a goal, or be possible. In fact, to highlight this greater context and analysis, alternative visual representations of this model show these orientations not on a continuum. In light of this, this model is useful in serving as a springboard for conversation about how an adult's orientation to cultural differences can affect their self-perception, and therefore their behavior in interacting with others. With respect to approaching race, I would continue to layer this understanding of intercultural development with concepts of inequity and systemic oppression that permeate through our lived experiences, compounded by bias and furthered by dominance of **White privilege,** and society's favoring of Whiteness. This will create a more holistic view of an individual's personal orientation toward differences, powerfully coupled with an awareness of historical and societal contextual factors that are extremely significant to a person's approach.

For the purposes of this conversation, the IDC model serves to illustrate the important notion that all adults are at very different places on the spectrum of cultural awareness and the capacity to navigate differences in an effective way. That is not to say that there cannot be movement among the different orientations, or that you may not adopt different approaches given a certain set of circumstances or topics. This model can underscore that although we do our best to access and engage in learning and teaching opportunities equally, it is erroneous to think a single approach to dealing with race and race conversations will work the same way for an individual in any family, household, or educational environment. This expectation *will set us up for failure,* as it doesn't allow for empathy and growth based on where an individual is at in their own personal journey of understanding about race.

The IDC demonstrates that there is a wide range in awareness of and capacity for navigating differences. This fundamental disposition among individuals is paramount in understanding one's approach to talking about cultural differences, including race.

It is important that we grasp these differences in intercultural development and our orientation toward differences as a precursor to any step forward toward racial awareness and understanding. Knowing this, we can better tailor learning opportunities and seek out resources at the appropriate level to meet the needs of any individual, group, or organization on this journey. It is also important to recognize these dynamics as affecting a person's path to nurturing racial identity development in children.

Teaching Tolerance

Teaching Tolerance[4] was founded in 1991 as a program of the Southern Poverty Law Center. This program is dedicated to reducing prejudice and improving intergroup relations in support of equitable school experiences for children. The program provides free resources, including a guide entitled "Let's Talk! Discussing Race, Racism and Other Difficult Topics with Students."[5]

This guide invites adults to go through a process of preparation before beginning to talk about race and **racism.** Although this resource is geared for educators, it can also be used by parents and caregivers who plan to discuss race topics in the home. These steps include

- **Assess your comfort level.** Face your own fears, address emotions and worries, and use methods that engage the conversation, rather than divert it.

- **Find comfort in discomfort.** Understand that feeling uncomfortable is normal, and practice facilitating difficult conversations and establishing community norms that can help support a healthy environment for dialogue.

- **Be vulnerable.** Reflect on what tends to take place for you during difficult conversations, especially focusing on vulnerabilities that may limit your effectiveness, and plan how to address these vulnerabilities.

- **Address strong emotions.** Recognize that speaking about race can elicit strong emotions both in the child and in yourself. Create a plan and identify strategies for how to respond to strong emotions such as pain/suffering/anger, blame, guilt, shame, and confusion or denial.

This guide by Teaching Tolerance includes graphic organizers to help guide your thinking and planning. I encourage you to utilize this guide and other free resources from this program and other organizations in order to aid in your preparation for having conversations about race.

Both the Intercultural Development Continuum and the Teaching Tolerance guide underscore how important it is for adults to recognize their own place on the journey of readiness for discussing or addressing racial differences, and to prepare for dialogue about race based on this awareness.

The journey in supporting multiracial and transracially adopted children starts with *you.*

Tools and Strategies for Talking about Race

We have just explored where you are on your journey of readiness to talk about race, and your approach to cultural differences. Taking this into consideration, the following are tools and strategies I have created to prepare for taking action in connecting with your child regarding race and their racial identity development. I call the capacity to engage with another person around topics of race "Racial Dialogue Readiness" (RDR). Let's begin with a reflection on your own Racial Dialogue Readiness.

Tool: Racial Dialogue Readiness (RDR): A Self-Reflective Questionnaire

Here is a list of questions to consider as you, and other adults around you, begin to explore race in your family or classroom. Moving through this reflection on your own will prepare you for conversations about race that you can participate in, to support your children.

1. How resolved am I with my own racial identity?
2. What fears do I have in talking about race? (e.g., fear of offending others, being judged, becoming emotional, etc.)
3. What bias (conscious and unconscious) do I have toward a particular group? What preferences do I have for one group or culture over another?

4. How objective can I be in talking about race overall, and about specific groups?

5. How have my lived experiences contributed to my conceptions of race?

6. What cultural heritage and ancestral lineage are an integral part of my frame of reference regarding race issues? What aspects of my cultural heritage and ancestral lineage do I want to learn more about?

7. Do I have unhealed trauma that may affect how able I am to approach a discussion or active exploration about race? What resources or action steps can support me with this?

8. Am I aware if my child or others around them have unhealed trauma that may affect how they approach a discussion or active exploration about race, and what is my reaction to that?

9. Do my partner, my family, or my colleagues have the same views toward race as I do? How does that affect me?

10. How do societal and political events affect my capacity and approach to discussing race with children?

11. What reading and other knowledge-gathering have I done on the topic at hand?

12. How ready am I to experience discomfort or challenge as we actively explore these topics?

13. How willing am I to acknowledge privilege and power dynamics in my analysis? How will I react when I delve deeper into how I may be complicit in upholding these dynamics through my own behaviors and actions?

14. What will I do if I am triggered in a conversation about race?

15. What will I do if I don't know the answer to a question?

16. Who can I rely upon for support for myself, as needed?

17. What resources and tools to support racial dialogue am I familiar with? What do I wish to learn more about?

As you consider these questions, celebrate strengths that you have in the richness you bring to the conversation. Also think about what can be done to alleviate any areas of concern. This careful approach and robust self-exploration can better prepare you for challenging conversations about race, because you held a mirror up to notice areas of strength and growth for you, in a balanced way.

Strategy: Addressing Your Intercultural Development Continuum (IDC) Orientation

The IDC orientations are a helpful benchmark in understanding where you or others may be on the continuum of intercultural development. But where do we go from there? It is important to consider what IDC orientation you may be demonstrating, and to think through how this could affect your care of a multiracial child.

Denial

If you, a family member, or a colleague is in denial about why racial differences exist or matter, it may be useful to do research on why this person has this perspective, and really examine how this may in fact impact your child. Is this due to the possibility that the person has lived isolated in a homogeneous group and is uninterested in acknowledging and experiencing difference? How is being around this viewpoint potentially affecting your multiracial child?

Polarization: Defense

If you tend to favor your culture over another culture, explore why that is. What is it about your culture that you identify with? What threat is there to accept and acknowledge the existence and validity of other cultures? Reflect on what series of events has led you to perceive other cultures in this way. Does your experience apply in all situations, and to all groups? How will your favoring of one culture impact the child, especially since their racial background consists of more than one culture? Notice how your interactions with your child may include this bias or preference.

Polarization: Reversal

You may be proud of your partner's culture or another culture that you have a particular affinity with, and reject your own culture. This can naturally happen if you have had a bad experience with your culture or people or communities within it, and choose to not be a part of that culture for related reasons. You may want to protect your child from the same negative experiences. Or perhaps you live in a new area or are a part of a cultural or faith-based community where you find you "click" with that culture more than your own. Notice if those tendencies are creeping into your conversations and other interactions with your child, and if they are picking up on those same preferences and norms. Reflect on how your multiracial child can appreciate your culture as well as another culture at the same time, since both are a part of their heritage.

Minimization

The intention behind treating "everyone the same" and the approach that "differences don't matter" is positive and inclusive-minded. That being said, there can be the danger of overlooking real differences in focusing too heavily on similarities. Practice noticing differences with your child in small ways. Reflect on how acknowledging differences can be empowering to increase under-standing of others and to increase the child's own self-confidence in being made up of multiple cultural heritages.

Acceptance

You may find yourself accepting differences but not knowing where to go next. Have conversations with the child reinforcing this accepting of multiple aspects of culture forming the child's identity at the same time. Attempt to introduce how differences can be a strength, and explore how to cultivate the strength of the diversity in your family, classroom, or community.

Adaptation

You or your child may be very able to navigate a variety of cultural situations with ease and natural effort. However, others may not be at the same place in their journey, and this can be challenging for you, requiring patience. Reflect on how to bring others along on this journey of cultivating acceptance, belonging, and active inclusion of cultural and racial differences. How can you reinforce this approach at home, at school, and in other parts of your child's daily life? Encourage learning moments as your child shares scenarios where they may need to process situations they face with others that test this sense of self-confidence and assurance about the benefit of differences and acknowledging all parts of one's identity, however they identify as a whole.

Overall, a deeper reflection into your Intercultural Development Continuum orientations will provide helpful knowledge about yourself and about others in your life. From there, you can pivot with action steps to help nurture the growth of your child's multiracial identity development.

Strategy: A New Model: Conscious Cultivation of Identity: The CCI Model

Through my experiences working with families and schools regarding talking about race, I have developed a model that may be helpful in supporting exploration and dialogue about race. This model can be helpful for introducing, examining, and affirming racial identity overall, and also within multiracial and transracially adopted children.

Conscious Cultivation of Identity (CCI) Model

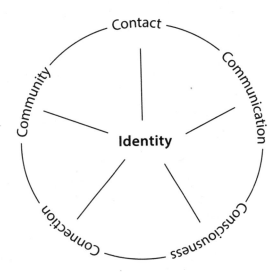

Figure 3. Conscious Cultivation of Identity (CCI) Model:
Contact, Communication, Consciousness, Connection, Community

I call this model "The Conscious Cultivation of Identity" (CCI), and it has five components: contact, communication, consciousness, connection, and community. It is especially important for multiracial individuals to have purposeful guidance about their multifaceted identity. As one Black and Japanese respondent shares, "I think discussions about identity would have been helpful growing up. Maybe not even discussions, but just a reminder from my parents that I come from two very different cultures and that I am a part of both, and that I shouldn't feel like I'm never enough for either one."

Contact

How can children learn knowledge of or pride in their own racial heritage if they don't have contact?

An Ethiopian and Chinese individual demonstrates this in her poignant experience of growing up:

> *I grew up in Asia until I was eight years old, so I had never seen another Black person outside of my family (dad and brother) before. My mom and Chinese grandmother were always the ones caring for my hair. This was something that is foreign to them, and they lacked the resources to help them maintain it properly, what to use to care for it, and ways to style it. In short, looking back now, I can say that I was deprived of what I needed to learn to embrace my curls.*

This contact starts at home and can continue in the classroom. The most direct source of having contact with culture comes from family members—but this may not be accessible to the child, depending upon the situation of the child and family (due to adoption, divorce, death, separation, shared custody, immigration, displacement, incarceration, estrangement, etc.). The next source of contact can come from friends and other community members, or even travel or attending festivals. This contact can be continued in the classroom through projects or dialogue that incorporate a celebration of a child's racial heritage that does not tokenize the child. This can include providing books, magazines, and videos about a child's cultural heritage—using credible sources, of course. This can also come in the form of exposure to art, music, dance, theater, photography, and other expressions of culture and race. When the teacher is proactive and allows for experiences with a child's racial and cultural heritage, the child will form an affinity for their racial group through positive associations and contact.

Communication

Contact with sources on culture and race is important, and communicating about this information is equally important, in order to deepen knowledge, understanding, and meaning about this contact. It is important to allow for the child to process their experiences as they come into contact with sources on their race and culture, in order to eventually be able to embody a definition of identity for themselves. It is important to provide context for the child as to what they are perceiving, and how differences manifest in themselves and are received in society. Can the child express aspects that make up their identity in a coherent way? This can of course evolve over time with age and cognitive development.

A Taiwanese and White individual shares, "When I was in high school one of my friends, who is also mixed, said that we aren't really Asian and that Asian people do not consider us Asian. And while I understand what she meant in that we did not grow up in Asia, and both Asian and White people see us as 'other,' it still kind of sent me into an identity crisis at that time. I felt like my mother's Asianness had influenced my perspective and experiences, so if I wasn't really Asian, what was I?" This example underscores how communication is incredibly important in fostering a healthy multiracial identity.

Consciousness

This expands communication about cultural and racial differences into the realm of discussing power and privilege dynamics, as well as how separation, isolation, marginalization, and oppression can exist due to race.

A European parent stated, "My husband is British–Trinidadian. Our young sons have an olive complexion and will likely be categorized as 'White.' I anticipate that our family's challenge will be in educating them about their multiethnic history and what that means, particularly as White privilege will be conferred upon them." This is where conscious dialogue can come in.

Although these can be difficult topics to delve into, children will be faced with these conversations at any age. It is important to be proactive and to find opportunities to expand the conversation in a constructive way that allows for critical thinking and a deeper analysis of these issues of equity and systemic bias. You can start to have gentle and then more forthright conversations about how these issues directly impact your child.

Connection

With all of the information and different experiences a child can face, it is essential to keep underscoring the importance of connection to their race and culture. It can be very tempting to distance oneself from a marginalized community if the recognition of oppression is overwhelming.

> *Growing up in a predominantly white and Latino community not knowing how to fit in was a daily struggle. I sadly learned very early on in life that code-switching and laughing along with borderline racist jokes were some of the things I had to do to be able to stay "normal" in school where there were little to no Asians and even fewer multiracial kids.*
>
> —*Filipino, Chinese, Belgian, Swedish individual*

Adults can buttress a perceived inferior sense of racial identity by offering positive examples of culture and race, to produce a larger picture rather than a negative image that can make anyone feel disengaged. Reiterating the connection to ancestors, contributions to society, beloved family members, friends, faith groups, festivals, the arts, and other aspects of culture and race can strengthen the bond the child has with their culture, to weather other aspects of the cultural experience that may challenge the child.

Community

It is essential to build a community of support and belonging around the child by creating or participating in spaces that are multiracial or that are tied to the child's own individual ethnic communities. This deepened relationship with community will help the child strengthen a bond to their own racial identity that can be done through external ties, but that is eventually internalized into a deeper feeling of appreciation within the child.

A Jewish parent shares their intentionality around building community: "My children are the other everywhere they go—with my white, Jewish family and with my husband's Kenyan family. We have sought out a community of other families who look just like ours so our kids can have a community of kids like them."

Creating community can be challenging in geographic regions that don't have the presence or an adequate number of children who reflect the same diversity as your own child, but gathering can be experienced in other ways. For example, you can take your child on a visit to a conference on multicultural education, culturally responsive teaching, or mindful parenting. Or you can expose the child to youth in another geographic region that more closely matches the identity of the child, through world or regional travel as a family, or by setting up a video classroom meeting with another school. You can join an online mixed race or transracial adoptee community and have discussions or show pictures of the multiracial and transracially adopted children that are posted in these groups. These community relationships certainly foster growth and awareness that allow the learning and understanding to happen outside of a family home or school classroom.

These tools and strategies are designed to "meet you where you are," drawing from a selection of models that may further awareness about a person's orientation toward addressing race and difference overall. Talking about cultural and racial differences is not easy—and there is an added complexity when teaching children. The purpose of this chapter is to acknowledge where an adult is, on their journey of comfort and awareness regarding holding racial dialogues; and to offer tools and strategies appropriate to one's place on that journey, in order to further reflection, conversation, and individual and collective action toward cultivating healthy and positive identities for multiracial and transracially adopted children.

3

Racial Rigidity, Fluidity, and Resilience

Far too often, race is examined and discussed along a Black and white binary, which leaves multiracial children feeling as though they do not have a place at the table. In order to strive for racial inclusion and justice, our conversations must include the nuances of multiracial identity.[1]

—LIZ KLEINROCK, educator, social justice
advocate, and founder of Teach and Transform

WHEN MY SON was six years old, he made a declaration in the car one day: "Mommy, you're white, and I am brown." I was sitting in the backseat beside him, and responded, "Actually, I'm Brown, and you're Brown too, and also White. In fact, Daddy is Brown and White also but most people don't notice that he's White." My younger son replied, "But does he get to choose?" My answer: "That's a great question...."

I could not help but notice my husband's raised eyebrows in the rearview mirror. Conversations about race can happen at any time, at any age, and especially when you're not expecting them!

This snippet illustrates how discussions about race can emerge. They can be organic and fleeting, and perhaps can catch us off-guard. In this example, I went on to explain further to my child about how our ethnic backgrounds relate to race and identity, and how perceptions of race by others can differ from what actually is the case, and also how you feel inside. This was not the first time we had talked about race and how we see ourselves, and definitely not the last. In later instances over months and years, I would see his understanding of race and physical representations of identity continue to form, based on the comments he makes about our skin color and how he notices it in other people or not. Over time, my children started to even notice when people are multiracial. As we read news pieces together, like a story of a win by Bubba Wallace, the NASCAR driver, I would state out loud, "Hmm, maybe he's biracial. What do you think?" And we would search online to learn more about his family. We also would have discussions about friends at school who are of multiple racial backgrounds, to enhance understanding of what the concept of multiracial means. This normalizes the idea of multiraciality and of talking about race in a nonstigmatized way. One can bring up race and multiracial identity in a way that is curious, positive, and nurturing—to discover more about the lives around us, and to show more of our multiracial children's identity in the world around them.

That being said, conversations about race without talking about systemic inequity present an incomplete picture of reality and can do harm because they can leave children unprepared when facing challenges or new awareness related to societal issues. It is important to teach our children and others around us how generations of systemic oppression and current **unconscious bias,** negative stereotyping, and explicit **discrimination** can and do happen due to race. The question is: how to delicately do this with children, without reinforcing **stereotypes** *or* a demoralizing sense of racial identity?

According to the National Institutes of Health,[2] **stereotype threat** occurs when "members of a marginalized group acknowledge that a negative stereotype exists in reference to their group, and they demonstrate apprehension about confirming the negative stereotype by engaging in particular activities." This is based on the research by Steele and Aronson[3] and later studies that show that individuals of color who were asked a demographic question about their race before taking a test underperformed compared with when they were not asked about their race prior to taking the test. This is due to negative generalizations about performance being primed in the individuals by the mere act of being questioned about and identifying with a certain racial identity. Stereotype threat creates a vulnerability and a risk of confirming this negative stereotype about one's group. This in turn causes underperformance or a lack of willingness to participate in an activity, due to this threat. Aligning with a stereotype creates a self-fulfilling prophecy of underperformance. For multiracial individuals, that can lead to a lack of wanting to identify with the group at all.

Adults who recognize and wish to address these negative generalizations about certain groups may attempt to remedy the discomfort of these negative stereotypes by telling a child, "We see this narrative about your group, but you're not one of them." Rather than picking apart the harmful generalization itself, the adult is elevating the child above the stereotype, indirectly saying, "You're better than the rest of your group"—yet the stereotype remains. This is called **exceptionalism.** What this does is create a dissonance between the child and the child's race, potentially causing the child to disown that part of their racial identity. Due to the bombardment of stereotypes within the media and institutional environments, multiracial children may also come to the conclusion on their own that dissociating with the part of themselves that is perceived as negative is a healthy choice, and a way to cope. Instead of choosing the marginalized identity, they may favor the other aspects of their identity that are aligned with the dominant culture, and that espouse privilege. For many individuals who live within a culture that privileges Whiteness, this could be a move to align with Whiteness while diminishing the relationship with their identity of color. An example of this could be a multiracial individual who is of Indian and White heritage experiencing and benefiting from light-skinned privilege in England, and therefore downplaying their South Asian heritage or even making fun of it when out with their White British friends. This is known as **internalized oppression** and can be directly tied to a **colonial mentality**[4] that permeates through many populations, including both the Filipinx and Pakistani sides of my family. The added complexity in this case is that the multiracial child may internalize oppression of one identity, and alleviate the pain and discomfort associated with that identity by favoring another one. The child's proximity to Whiteness and ability to reap the privileges and safety associated with that would reinforce her dismissing or hiding her South Asian heritage.

I mention safety because sometimes the decision to express one identity more than another is due to the potential for experiencing societal violence or harm, in just living out one's full heritage. As a young person fresh out of college, I had a supervisor at an educational institution who, after finding out that my father was Pakistani, said, "I'm sure he's not a terrorist like the al-Qaeda." This was a serious comment directed at me in conversation, not one of humor or lightheartedness, nor subtly mentioned in passing. Was this statement racist? Or was this person genuinely trying to connect with me by complimenting my family? Or both? This is a classic example of when well-meaning adults say, "Oh, you're not one of *them*." As a young person and just starting out in my career, I was ill-prepared to adequately address this message in a work setting as it took me by surprise. Additionally, the power hierarchy present with this person being an authority figure paralyzed me from really doing anything about it. As a multiethnic individual, I chose to respond to that moment by downplaying my Pakistani and Muslim heritage by focusing on things that were commonplace in mainstream national culture, and also by highlighting my Filipina heritage—which is perceived by others as "friendly" and unthreatening in most circumstances. Sadly, there were many moments growing up when I did this repeatedly, as Islamophobia and negative representations of Muslims and people from the region of Pakistan as terrorists are rampant in the news and in mainstream entertainment. My method was to align myself with other identities rather than face the awkward and uncomfortable situations that came with such challenges. These experiences used to bring me shame in multifold ways: shame for *being* my identity, and then also shame for *hiding* it. Looking back now with full pride in all of my identities offers me a renewed perspective about how these external factors caused my choice of identity preferences and resulted in this behavior. This reflection and deeper understanding also motivate me to bring about awareness to this issue, and to share with others my story of resilience.

Downplaying a part of one's identity by multiracial individuals can also occur in many geographic areas with any dominant **monoracial** majority culture that is reinforced in society, media, and a region's institutions. An example of this is a multiracial teenager who is Black and Japanese living in Japan who focuses on **performing** Japanese identity by straightening their hair or using skin lightening products to hide their Blackness—which one can argue is still espousing the idea of aligning with White privilege as Asian identities are perceived to be closer to White identities than are Black identities. This focusing and performing of one part of a person's identity over another can also lead to shame within the multiracial individual when it is made apparent in social or family situations or in public settings that there are other aspects of their racial identities that are undesired or unvalued.

The phenomenon of a multiracial individual attempting to align with the dominant culture can also exist within monoracial or monoethnic communities that are not White. This outcome is not limited to environments that value Whiteness as superior.

For example, students may feel pressured to embody a single cultural heritage and identity and participate in activities emphasizing this, rather than be open about expressing their multiracial identity. An example of this is a multiracial Italian/Irish, Jamaican/Chinese student who shares her experience in university: "I also faced the challenge of never being 'enough' of one thing to significantly feel a part of a group. In college I even attended an orientation for a sorority for students of color. When I arrived, the women who were there had primarily darker African skin tones and I had awkward conversations and felt like I had to justify being there."

Another instance is a mixed race youth who grew up embracing both Filipinx and Latinx cultures, and was able to speak Tagalog and Spanish. However, when they started school, this changed: "I was always seen as an impostor by both sides. My Spanish wasn't good enough to be Mexican. I didn't grow up in a rich family like other Filipinos. I learned, ultimately, that I had to come into myself and not check all the boxes that others or myself have created to identify myself as a real Filipino or Mexican."

Some youth may choose the action of **covering,** or hiding of their full and authentic self in order to fit in. This very real phenomenon can contribute to feelings of **racial imposter syndrome** for multiracial individuals, related to trying to fit in with any one culture. Multiracial individuals may also be accused of **cultural appropriation** of certain cultural elements, including customs and practices, clothing, and hairstyles, because others may not view them as belonging to the culture in question!

Another individual who identifies as Filipino and White shares, "I deal with racial impostor syndrome—not feeling like I fit in with White people, not feeling like I fit in within the Filipino community in my city. I'm afraid to meet other Filipinos my age because I'm afraid they're going to reject me. I constantly feel lost and disconnected. I fear that it is too late for me to claim my Filipino culture and identity because I didn't when I was a child and teenager so that would make me a fraud."

A contributing element to this complex dynamic is that members of the marginalized community may notice a multiracial person's fluidity or ability to choose identity, and "call out" the person for trying to "pass" for another heritage and positioning themselves to gain privilege by "not owning" the part of themselves that society deems as valued less. Again, rather than focus on the systemic factors that contribute to an unhealthy relationship with that part of one's identity as the root cause for this phenomenon, a common reaction by others may be to blame the multiracial individuals *themselves* for attempting to navigate this dynamic and hierarchy in the way that they have discovered is possible and seems to work well for them as a coping strategy, in the absence of being able to be accepted as multiracial. We must note that this blame and calling out come from a cycle of pain and trauma that is felt by marginalized communities, and speaking to that pain is empowering and acknowledging of the systemic oppression that occurs due to race. That being said, the cycle of harm and pain continues when this is directed at multiracial individuals, who are also a recipient of othering and exclusion in this process—by more than one group.

Finally, what about parents' and caregivers' role in this? Parents' and caregivers' modeling of racial identity can play a direct role in how a child views race overall, as well as their own identity. If a parent or caregiver is forthright in discussing race in a positive, proactive way, children will have the opportunity to formulate ideas with gentle guidance from parents and caregivers. This doesn't mean the parent/caregiver has to have all the answers; it can be a journey of discovery and exploration for both the child and the adult at the same time. In contrast, some parents and caregivers may have so much internalized oppression that they will go to the extent of hiding parts of their racial identity from their children, only to have the children find out later about it. I met a woman who was Mexican and Italian who was only told about her Mexican heritage by her mother on her deathbed. She had lived her entire life not knowing she was Mexican. Until this day, she is still "read" as White and claims her Italian heritage publicly, not her Mexican heritage. It's helpful to examine what societal forces may have caused this decision to hide one's identity, rather than focus on it solely as an individual choice. How do societal conceptions of race shape a child's experience of and connection to it?

Many parents and caregivers may choose to celebrate a child's multiple heritages by exposing them to cultural festivals or family gatherings where a child can learn about the various aspects of their identity through being in community with others. This can help children define their racial identity in a way that grows a linkage to it in a positive and concrete way. In contrast, a parent from a marginalized community may choose to downplay one aspect of their racial heritage by avoiding family members and community groups where that culture is found, or by denouncing the entire community as being inferior, as a result of internalizing the overall oppression of that group that they have been exposed to. Further, a parent may access the privilege from their partner's dominant identity or adopt their partner's culture and shed their own by distancing themselves from their own history or language. Children who are brought up in this environment will undoubtedly inherit some of these characteristics of hiding, shame, or distancing. However, the child may grow to develop interest in that identity and begin a search for or further exploration into more aspects of their identity when they are able to as they get older. Some parents resist this, and older multiracial children have yet *another* layer to navigate, this time of needing to reassure their parents about *their* identity choices and journey, as the children continue the exploration themselves.

As we can see, there can be a range of outcomes for the child based on the setting they are raised in, and how their experiences of race are handled within the family environment. There are also more circumstances that can be at play than have been mentioned in these immediate examples, thereby leading to an even more varied range of outcomes. There is no singular experience that is the same for all multiracial children except for the need to balance a variety of inputs that inform a child's racial identity.

Most of this dynamic is happening so subconsciously that the parties involved (multiracial individuals, adult caregivers, peers, community leaders) do not recognize the intricacies of this cycle and the added complexities of the multiracial component of identity. A positioning of the benefits of multiraciality may simply be seen by others as elevating multiracial individuals "above" or "beyond" inferior races, especially in a racial climate marked by the binary of "us versus them." This perceived posturing creates a division for multiracial people between themselves and many other groups and individuals—including family members and friends. This is the danger when being multiracial is showcased or is perceived as being superior. If society and adults are telling multiracial youth to "rise above" the stereotypes of their perceived "inferior" racial identity without teaching about systemic inequity, there may also be individuals from monoracial identity groups pointing out the fluidity of identity as privileging the multiracial experience. Monoracial individuals may also perceive that multiracial individuals are "reaping the benefits" of more than one identity, whenever it is convenient.

The added layer of complexity of a multiracial person not completely fitting in as a person of color yet also not fully realizing the identity of being White, or not fully belonging within *any* monoracial identity, leaves individuals in a space where they may feel a complete lack of belonging or inclusion. If not accepted fully by any of their communities without having to completely adopt the ways of those groups, where do multiracial people fit in? A person who identifies as Filipino, Hawaiian, Native American, and White shares a touching account of what this is like:

> *Not brown enough to fit in with my brown side and friends (Filipino, Hawaiian, Native) and yet too ethnic to fit in with my white friends and family. White family commenting on my skin, hair, etc., and referring to me as the brown girl. Brown friends calling me the browbeat white girl they know, etc. You just never fit in anywhere. But my soul yearns for my Filipino and Hawaiian side the most, yet I feel like when I'm repping that side of me or partaking in those cultural activities I feel like I'm a phony or appropriating the culture.*

I have coined the term "multiracial identity quagmire" to describe this experience of when a multiracial person doesn't feel that they fit in *anywhere*. This is something multiracial children must navigate with little to no direct guidance from mainstream sources about the complex and layered experience they are having. As one Egyptian and Mexican individual describes, "My entire life no one knew what I was. I was never accepted in any group."

Instead, a multiracial person may be offered the option to identify with one side of their identity or another. Or they could be exposed to the idea of multiraciality being accepted, or even "cool" or a "fun blend"—in order to value "mixedness" in a mainstream, acceptable way that is what I call **multiracial positive.** Similar to how the terms "body positive" or "sex positive" invoke "positivity" movements, the term **multiracial positivity** describes the social movement that promotes a positive sense of self around multiracial identity. This can be seen in the plethora of media content or fashion apparel that promotes the multiracial and the mixed experience, which has grown over the years. These positive conceptions of multiraciality are in direct contrast with historical, negative narratives of multiracial people being the "tragic mulatto" or facing a crisis as they uncover their mixed heritage.

Although positivity about multiraciality is a step in the right direction, there is the danger of keeping awareness and analysis at a superficial level, which can objectify and exotify multiracial children. One should proceed with caution when stating objectifying sentiments such as "All mixed people are better looking" or "Multiracial people have hybrid vigor," as they are problematic attempts at being multiracial positive but can do damage as they espouse superiority of multiraciality without meeting the need for a deeper understanding of, conversation about, and strategies for how to face issues that are specific to multiracial individuals. One should not exhibit multiracial positivity in ways that are at the expense of our monoracial colleagues, family, and community members. This is because multiracial positive behaviors and expression can be misconstrued as marginalizing and othering monoracial people, even though this is not intended. As we can see, this dynamic is extremely complex and sensitive. This is where parents, caregivers, and educators can come in—to scaffold that exploration in a purposeful, healthy, and positive way that promotes self-discovery, reflection, and understanding of identity in a way that is developmentally appropriate for the child.

How to Have a Conversation about Race and Multiraciality

Does talking about race create more stigmas? This very concern is why many, many parents, caregivers, and educators choose not to focus on race or discuss it at all. The thought and belief are that focusing on race will only lead to further racialization in children's minds. The fact is, though—that if parents, caregivers, and educators don't take hold of the conversation and create a more holistic sense of the issue—a child's understanding of race will be filled in solely with incomplete or inaccurate depictions and understandings of race from peers, the media, and society. This is a dangerous proposition for our valued group—our children.

Also, it is important to talk with children not only about race, but about multiracial identity specifically. As professor and researcher Dr. Sarah Gaither states:

> *There is a lot of work looking at how parents within racial and ethnic minority families socialize and prepare their own children for bias since those parents growing up as Black or Latino (as examples) know what types of experiences their children may face. However, there is far less work examining how parents of multiracial children socialize their kids. What makes this so unique is a monoracial parent, even if a racial minority, does not necessarily know what types of questions or identity denial experiences their child may face. U.S. society also essentializes race, meaning we think very fixed about belonging to just one racial group, but multiracial children defy that default categorical view. That is what makes raising a multiracial child so difficult at times, is the variation that comes with which racial or ethnic identity is most salient.[5]*

How do we go about beginning a discussion? A process that may be helpful in supporting multiracial identity in children involves noticing, destigmatizing, building conceptions of, and focusing on racial identity. At home, this can be taking the approach to have healthy conversations about these topics, even when different family members may have varying conceptions toward race and identity. In the classroom, these are helpful strategies for all children, as they model how a conversation about race does not have to be charged—and can be one of observation, curiosity, and awareness-building.

- **Noticing Race.** Ask the child: What do you notice about your race? How do you see yourself? How is this different from or the same as how others see you?

  This step is essential as it encourages adults leading the conversation to go beyond skipping past opportunities to engage about race, and to dive deeper instead. This engagement can arise in dialogue naturally, or can be initiated by the adult with the child in the context of a larger conversation. I recommend being proactive so that you are prepared for the discussion and can guide your child in their understanding in a developmentally appropriate way, and so there is a positive foundation before they encounter a negative incident.

- **Destigmatizing Race.** Ask: What negative stereotypes about race exist? How are these untrue or are the outcome of systemic oppressive practices and policies? What are the sources of these stereotypes? How can we overcome these negative stereotypes, through critical reflection or other actions?

  As was mentioned previously, a common trigger for talking about race and ethnicity is a negative comment or encounter experienced by your child. If that happens, immediately address that specific incident, and use it as a foundation for looking at the world with a critical eye. Relating a specific troubling moment to larger aspects of inequity can help children understand that it isn't their fault, and they need not feel badly or ashamed.

> **Building Racial Identity.** Ask: What are some positive conceptions of your race? How can we work to dismantle the negative narratives in favor of positive ones? What do you know about yourself that others don't know?

Surrounding your child with positive conceptions of their racial heritage is essential to help reinforce a healthy and connected sense of identity. Showing movies, reading books, attending community festivals, and having friends from the same racial and cultural background can fill a child with positive associations that can build their own identity. This may mean expanding your and their friend circle to meet other individuals who are both from the same racial background or who are multiracial themselves. This can foster a sense of normalcy and pride for the child, in seeing themselves out in the world.

> **Focusing on Multiracial Identity.** Discuss with the child: What does your multiracial identity mean to you? How does it feel to be a part of more than one group at the same time? Do you prefer to balance your identities or choose one more than the other? Why is that?

Exploring multiracial identity specifically will honor the different aspects of the child that co-exist at the same time. Be purposeful in recognizing the child's multiracial background and explain how there are different parts of a child's heritage that exist, and a combined identity that can feel different from each part. Utilize some of the resources listed in chapter 9 of this book to spark thought about multiracial identity and to build the conversation.

ACTIVITY: BECAUSE I AM …

A great activity to start a conversation with your child about noticing race, countering stereotypes, and building a positive sense of multiracial identity is to play a game of storytelling using this prompt:

"Because I am …, people think …"

You can go first, modeling something non-race-related to kick off the conversation. For instance, "Because I am tall, people think I am a basketball player," or "Because I am a woman, people think I am a great cook." There might be a natural conversation where your child can ask "Why?" and you can explain about people's thoughts and how these perceptions are not true in every case. This naturally leads to a discussion about bias and stereotyping without even needing to use those terms!

When it's the child's turn, notice what they say about themselves, and try to further the conversation using prompts and questions.

They may say, "Because I am lighter than my mom, people think she is my nanny." You can ask, "Who thinks that about you?" "How do you know they think that way?" "How do you feel about that impression?" Really dig in to identify the source of the impression—is it friends, family members, the teacher, strangers? You will learn about the child's world from their perspective, and they will know that you care and are listening and may have some suggestions for how to deal with those situations.

For younger children, you can change the prompt to address traits they possess by saying, "Because I have." Your child may say, "Because I have dark skin, people think I'm not from this country" or "Because I have a strange name that is hard to pronounce, people think I'm different and don't want to be my friend." Again, follow up with further questions about how they think and feel, so that you can respond to them with a fuller sense of the situation.

You can have this dialogue on a regular basis and see how their answers change at specific ages or periods of their life. Notice any differences that have come due to any changes to geographic locations, friends they are with, activities they are involved with, or teachers or coaches they are exposed to. Feel free to keep a journal of the discussion and your child's responses. This will provide much insight into their thoughts about their identity during their years of growth and development.

4

Factors Impacting Racial Identity Choice and Assignment

WHEN MY GRANDMOTHER passed away, it was a soul-crushing moment for me. She had lived with our family starting when I was a very young child. Originally from India, she moved to Pakistan to be married, and gave birth there to my father and four other children. She had a third grade education. She was staunch in her ways, both culturally and religiously. I learned tremendously through her about that side of my culture, including how to cook, speak the language, pray, and generally—how to be. Soon after she died, I remember looking at a rolling pin I had in my kitchen cupboard, wondering if I could ever make roti as well as she did. Even as I write this, it brings tears to my eyes.

Processing these moments further, I realized in addition to missing her physical presence in my life, her absence exemplified to me a severing of a connection to South Asian culture in its entirety, as my finest teacher about it was now gone. How would I ever fully learn everything it means to be South Asian, and continue to be accepted by the community, without her guiding me? Identity for me, and for many multiracial individuals, is a lifelong process of learning and experiences involving a combination of choice and assignment. What are factors that impact this journey of racial identification? How do inputs from and biases of others impact a child's choice and experience of identity? What must we be aware of, in how exposure and reinforcement to culture and communities are active determinants of identity for our children?

Proving Racial Legitimacy

The experience of needing to prove one's connection to a culture or race is the idea of proving **racial legitimacy.** Another way to put this is the need to respond in some way to the underlying senti-ment faced by multiracial people and other individuals whose race may not match others' perceptions of them, when others call out the challenge: "Are you _____ enough?" This question alludes to the demand of having to legitimize one's identity by answering the question "Are you enough of a culture or race to claim that?" and the following charge: "Prove it."

For my previous book *Being All of Me,*[1] I designed an activity called the "Multiracial Yardstick" where individuals can plot questions they are constantly asked, such as "Do you speak the lan-guage?" "Have you ever been to that country?" "Do you like the food?" of each culture. With each question, multiracial people are challenged with proving racial legitimacy. The point of this activity is to highlight to children how racial identity measurement occurs, the process of inclusion and exclusion that takes place, and how to potentially address it.

A Black, Filipino, and Mexican individual shares their experi-ence with the yardstick:

Sometimes people would quiz me on historical, cultural, or language stuff and it was as if they were trying to measure how much of an ethnicity I was. This type of stuff came from older family members and friends. If I got the answers correct, they would say something like "You're a true Filipino," etc. I pass the test so then I don't get excluded. I remember some older cousins spoke Tagalog really fast and asked me, "What did I say?" I answered correctly so I was in the in crowd. This isn't just an experience I've had in just Filipino; it has happened with me in my Black ethnicity too, like there are measures if you can dance or sing you're in, if not you're out.

In the same vein, having immediate or extended family members of the culture in question can support a child's sense of belonging in that culture. It is racial legitimacy by proxy. A multiethnic Chinese and European person may embody the response: "You don't think I'm Chinese enough? Well, look at my Chinese aunts who still live in China today. There. I have proven myself." A biracial Latinx and White person may show a picture of immediate family members on their phone to questioning colleagues, or express what music they listen to or food that they eat, in order to show their connection to either of their cultures.

This questioning of proving racial legitimacy can be hard on a child who is merely aiming to fit into school and society overall, without the added burden of having to prove how entrenched they are in a specific culture. The growing pains of child and adolescent development are difficult enough, and are exacerbated by this additional challenge. The same Black, Filipino, and Mexican respondent describes the feelings behind this experience so well: "Being multiethnic, people are always trying to measure you, your features, knowledge, and they make up their own percentages about you from their false percepts. I don't want to be measured, only accepted."

The complexity of addressing racial legitimacy can also be intensified when the child lives with one parent and not the other, or lives far away from the other members of their family who represent the part of the culture being questioned. The result can be either a distancing from one of their racial identities or an internal struggle to connect with the race or culture that is not present. The challenge of racial identification and proving legitimacy can definitely be a primary concern for a child who is a transracial adoptee—a person who is adopted and whose racial heritage is different from their parents'. Needing to prove racial legitimacy is especially present when a child looks physically different from one of the races that they identify with. We will explore this particular aspect of identity further in this chapter as we discuss phenotype, or physical appearance.

A person who has Filipino–Chinese–European heritage describes their experience of proving racial legitimacy: "Many ask if I can speak Tagalog, and when I answer that I can only speak at the tourist level (ordering food, giving directions, etc.), the response is usually a mix of disappointment and judgment."

The questioning of legitimacy can come from others around the child, but can also come from within. Many a time the thoughts and curiosity about one's culture or racial heritage can come from children themselves as they explore the meaning of their own identity. When that happens, what structures are in place to support that learning? How can adults and caregivers surrounding the child scaffold learning about the culture and identification related to race?

Exposure and Reinforcement

You may find the burden of responsibility is given to the immediate caregiver to expose the child to different aspects of culture. This can be especially challenging when there is a need for teaching about a culture that may not be one that the caregiver belongs to themselves. Ways to do this would be to involve the child in local community or cultural festivals and programs, take trips to the child's country of origin, or expose them to religious or cultural centers or neighborhoods where this culture can be found thriving naturally. This active exposure to culture and added involvement by the parents can help support the child's learning about their own cultural heritage and racial background.

However, what if these things are not available to the child? What if the parent or caregiver is not active in taking action in this way?

My research on family communication patterns of multiethnic individuals[2] demonstrated what can happen when the reinforcement is not initiated within the family.

One child who has a Filipina mother and a White father grew up with his father as his parents were divorced. His physical appearance was that he had darker skin and darker hair—he visibly looked multiracial and not completely White-passing as an individual. I vividly recall in my interview of him how he talked negatively about Filipinx people, saying how they are "lower class" and "only worked in fast-food joints." It was shocking to me to see how he visibly exhibited characteristics of being Filipino, and was Filipino himself, but had grown to have a negative conception of that part of his identity.

The same thing can happen through lack of contact with a particular part of a child's identity. The child may grow distant and detached from that identity, and this lack of understanding may be filled in with other sources of information or opinions from the rest of society or the child's surroundings—which can be positive or negative, accurate or inaccurate, in conceiving of the culture.

If a child physically looks like one part of their heritage and doesn't learn much about the other, it may be in alignment and not cause any conflict, as the identification is clear and reinforced by external perceptions and reactions, as well as internal family dynamics. I met a couple with children, and the father's mother is from Myanmar (formerly known as Burma) and the father's father is from England. He married someone from Scotland and their children have a British last name and look White. Because of the trauma of civil war that happened in Myanmar and the intense loss and death that the father's family experienced, he has chosen to not teach his children about it. The children have therefore not learned much about their Burmese heritage and phenotypically look White and have a British last name. How they identify is congruent with their physical characteristics, and with other social markers such as name, and is reinforced by how they are raised by both parents. There is no question of racial legitimacy in this case.

That being said, a different family with a similar background may choose to instill a sense of connection to more than one ethnic heritage. There may be more tension in endeavoring to reinforce this identity especially if there is not a physical match with the child's appearance—this is where the call for proving racial legitimacy may come in. Understanding these aspects of racial identification leads us to consider how physical appearance can play a critical, mitigating role in the experience of a racialized identity.

Phenotype and Assignment

There is added complexity to identifying with a particular race when a child phenotypically looks like the part of their identity that they have grown distant from, and yet society treats them that way based on their physical appearance. The child may reject these conceptions by others, and go through turmoil trying to prove themselves different from these perceptions.

Another instance could be when a child doesn't look like the group they feel close to, and has to constantly prove that they are "down with the community" that they are trying to belong to.

Both of the above scenarios can cause tension in a person's sense of self as they are rejected by one group, or are assigned membership to another group, and strive to be accepted as how they see themselves in reality. This questioning of racial legitimacy can be a struggle for youth, all the way through to adulthood. Sometimes a particular BIPOC racial or cultural group can have bias against another racial or cultural group or toward members of their own racial group, even when they are not White. This is called **horizontal racism**[3] and can feel like a betrayal by one's group, creating even more pressure for multiracial individuals to try to belong to a particular race or culture. How can caregivers and educators support this learning and identity development while all of this is going on for children?

Classroom Environment

Educators who teach children about the multiple possibilities of identity—be it race, gender, or language—are likely to create classroom and school environments that are more accepting of and inviting to a spectrum of identity, rather than a fixed sense of identity. This is especially important as multiracial children go through an exploration of what this means to them. By making sure members of the classroom are all on the same page about topics and terminology, and taking classmates through identity-exploring activities all together as a group, there can be a sense of relief for the multiracial student—because they won't stand out on this journey of exploration and uncertainty.

Home Environment

It may behoove parents to be proactive in exposing their children to various cultures that their children belong to. This can call for extra effort when that culture is different from the parents' own cultural and racial heritage. Exposing children to aspects of their culture that support their learning can be instrumental in creating a healthy sense of self for our children, and can prevent tension from not knowing parts of oneself, thereby forcing children to reject parts of themselves.

Empowerment and Choice

Another contributing factor to a child's racial identification is when a parent does not want their child to acknowledge parts of their identity. This can come from trauma due to what that identity represents, namely: rejection from extended family belonging to that community, intersection with social class or other elements that the parent is trying to distance their family from, or the parent's feelings of wanting the child to accept the parent as an individual and reject others. This confluence of variables can impact the environment of upbringing that the child has. This context is duly important for educators and others around the child to understand, acknowledge, and respect.

In contrast with positioning a singular sense of identity upon our children, we can reinforce the idea of choice as an option for them.

A very powerful explanation of choice about racial identity for multiracial individuals was developed by Dr. Maria P. P. Root and is called the "Bill of Rights for Racially Mixed People."[4]

This Bill of Rights expresses the ability of a racially mixed person to have choice, and to understand how that choice may change over time and may be different from the choices of other family members or others in their school or community who may have the same ethnic background. It can be used as a guide for discussions with fellow adults in your family, school, or community. It can also invite self-reflection on your part as a caregiver, challenging assumptions about race being a static concept, defined by set criteria.

ACTIVITY

Read the following "Bill of Rights for Racially Mixed People." Note your reactions to each of these statements. In particular, note

🐾 Do you have strong feelings toward any of these statements? What comes up for you? What about the particular statement is provoking?

🐾 Are there positions regarding racial identification that you disagree with? Haven't experienced or cannot relate to? Haven't thought of?

🐾 Which of these statements may hold true for your child, but not for you or others in your family? Which of these differ from your own experiences, or experiences of members of your school and general community?

Bill of Rights for Racially Mixed People

By Maria P. P. Root

I HAVE THE RIGHT ...

Not to justify my existence in this world.

Not to keep the races separate within me.

Not to be responsible for people's discomfort with my physical ambiguity.

Not to justify my ethnic legitimacy.

I HAVE THE RIGHT ...

To identify myself differently than strangers expect me to identify.

To identify myself differently from how my parents identify me.

To identify myself differently from my brothers and sisters.

To identify myself differently in different situations.

I HAVE THE RIGHT …

To create a vocabulary to communicate about being multiracial.

To change my identity over my lifetime—and more than once.

To have loyalties and identification with more than one group of people.

To freely choose whom I befriend and love.

> *Maria P. P. Root, PhD, is author of* Racially Mixed People of America.

This Bill of Rights underscores the idea of choice and the fluidity of a changing identity over time.

One issue that may arise with respect to choice about racial identification is that parents may choose an identity for their child, reinforce it, and feel a sense of rejection if this changes later in life.

For example, a parent who is African American may underscore the heritage of a biracial child identifying as Black from a very young age, telling her that this is how people will perceive her, and how she will be treated in society, and that she should be proud of it. Phenotypically, the child looks like a lighter-skinned Black child through her physical appearance and the texture of her hair. The child may grow up with a Black racial identity reinforced by who she is exposed to in her friend group, or at school, and overall by society. However, she may go away to college and meet friends who are of different ethnic backgrounds, including those who are White, like the other part of her identity. She may explore being around these individuals and feel a sense of unfamiliarity at first, and confusion because of this identity not being an option for her since birth. There may be feelings of questioning or guilt as to how to accept all parts of herself and be comfortable in doing that. How can she have pride in being Black, but then also accept the Whiteness that is a part of her? How can she be seen as legitimate by **social justice** movements in society that support equity and justice for Black lives, when she is also White, and there is an active push against **White supremacy** from her Black friends that alienates her White friends? Does she really belong in any group? What is her true identity? What stand should she take?

The solo show by Fanshen Cox called *One Drop of Love* artistically navigates the push and pull of changing identity in Fanshen's own personal story navigating biracial identity. How are the legitimacy of her actions and her involvement on behalf of the Black community respected, accepted, or challenged when she is also White? How much does one accept oneself, as a part of one group or another, in any given moment? There are so many layers to how an individual grows and develops their identity, especially within new environments and as they are surrounded by different groups. This show is an example through performance that highlights the fluidity of identity and also the challenge that may come from others in their perceptions of how that identity should be lived.

Efforts that polarize racial groups, including historical conflict among different cultures, are extremely difficult for individuals of multiracial backgrounds to navigate. It can be difficult for adults of monoracial heritage—so imagine children of multiracial backgrounds.

Through my time reading about, researching, and interacting with individuals of different cultures, it is clear that the tensions among historically polarized groups also add an extra layer of pressure on children who come from those groups. For example, someone who is Vietnamese and White may feel torn about the Vietnam War, and the political positioning and rhetoric about what took place in history, due to their ability to see both sides of this conflict. It can be alarming and confusing for a child to be a product of two societies that were formally at war, are currently embroiled in battle, or are in opposition.

Parents, caregivers, and educators reading this book may feel strongly about a child identifying one way or another, or encompassing all identities. That is the power of this conversation—to highlight that this can be different for different people. Not all multiracial individuals identify the same way, and not all parents raise their multiracial children the same way. As a result of their upbringing early on, and exposure to different experiences and environments later in life, children may go through a period of *rejecting the identity that was chosen for them early in life.* Children later on may feel ashamed of being different and may hide parts of themselves to fit in. Or they may feel proud of and in alignment with choosing all or parts of their racial identity to fully embody. All of these outcomes are possible and can continue to be in flux throughout adulthood. At some point, conceptions of identity begin to harden and become fixed. Whether it is an affinity with one group over another, or the idea that identity can flux in different situations—as individuals grow older, they tend to subscribe to an identity that suits them.

Kip Fulbeck's book and powerful exhibit on Hapa identity[5] demonstrate the phenomenon of differences in racial identification both across individuals and within individuals over time, through photos. In this exhibit and book that capture pictures of multiracial individuals and asked the subjects of each photo to write a description of themselves to put beside the photo, one can see the range of identities that have been formed, assigned, or chosen. These include:

- Being more aligned with one aspect of identity over others

- Rejecting the need to choose a racial category—saying, "I am human"

- Embracing all aspects of the parts of one's identity

- Embodying a "multiracial" or "mixed" or "other" identity as a whole sense of self that doesn't fit into a box

- Being called to identify with aspects of identity other than race—e.g., gender, geographic location, military status, etc.—more so than racial background

- Not being sure yet but identifying in a certain direction, for now

The descriptions by children are especially fascinating as some drew pictures or talked about feelings to describe their identities.

The gift of Kip's exhibit was that he did it again fifteen years later, and compared descriptions of a selection of people, seeing how they identified stayed the same or changed over time.

One of these individuals, Dr. Curtiss Takada Rooks, who is of Japanese and African American heritage, was a part of both exhibits. Reflecting on his own multiracial identity, he says,

Often in an effort of sensitivity and support people have said to me, "It must have been **hard** *growing mixed." Even when I was an adolescent, this declaration of* **hardness** *seemed "off." At that point, I could not articulate why it felt disquieting. In reflection, of then and now, it was because it inferred an "easy" existence, that is, if I was not mixed then my growing up would have been easy.*

*Moreover, it seemed to imply that I had a
choice "of being mixed." Even if I choose or
am forced, to identify primarily with one or the
other of my mixes, I know that I am mixed.
I saw my mixedness every morning when I
looked at my parents at breakfast. I saw my
mixedness every time I looked in the mirror.
Growing up mixed was and is, an "is." A
more complex is, but an "is" nonetheless.*[6]

Curtiss relates his own understanding of multiracial identity to that of parenting mixed race children, saying:

*... The complexities lie not **within** the mixed race
child, but is imposed externally in the ways that
society imagines the mixed race child. Navigating
the general society, along with the various communities into which the mixed race child is born
creates a web of complexities. The mixed race child
becomes the literal body in which the society's
struggles with race, culture, ethnicity and hege-
mony gets played out. We at once become all that
is hopeful, and all that is feared, by "race mixing."
Such negotiation and navigation, however, is the
"is" of our lives. Recognizing and accepting this
complexity allows us (the mixed race person) to
realize "our normal." And, it is in our comfort
with "our normal" that makes it "easy."*

*Because of the ways in which societies
imagine the mixed race person, parenting
of mixed race children must take on
an intentionality about race.*

As described in this quotation, there must be an intentionality on the part of the parents to "face race" and teach multiracial children about their racial identity. The following are some strategies to cultivate a healthy, full sense of self among multiracial individuals:

- Expose them to different parts of their cultures.

- Help them understand that differences are to be celebrated, are not just "normal" or "acceptable" in us. Differences are not just good—they're *great*!

- Emphasize that different people choose to identify in different ways.

- Realize that groups don't all get along with one another, and historical and current tensions can be present among groups, including the groups the child is a part of in their own identities.

- Explain that others may see the child differently or the same as the child sees themselves, at any given moment.

- The child may identify differently from siblings or other family members, and this may change over time.

- The parent, caregiver, or educator accepts the choices the child makes now and in the future.

- There may be a variety of feelings associated with figuring out the child's identity, and that is also welcomed and accepted as part of the process.

- Expose them to communities and ideas of being multiracial as an option in their growth process.

Interference by Gatekeepers

One important question remains: who gets to be the "gatekeeper" of identity? With any culture, there tend to be individuals who chime with their opinion as to the appropriate expression of a person's culture or identity. The benefit of this is that they reinforce, affirm, and teach aspects of the culture that the child may not know. The downside of this is that this may seem like "policing" of an individual's expression of their identity, through monitoring how their clothes, hair, or way of walking or talking is done. When allowed to denigrate a child's expression of identity, these gatekeepers can destroy a child's self-confidence and fluidity of identity, because the child succumbs to the criticism of the gatekeeper's opinions of how to express one's racial heritage. Although there may be good intentions to the gatekeeper's actions—in upholding and reinforcing the expression of identity in its "pure" form—this can go counter to supporting a multiracial child's individual exploration and expression of identity in the way that is possible for them, or in a way that they choose.

The resulting corrective actions can take place in the form of admonishing on social media of how a person looks or talks, or a polite hint at a family gathering, or direct commentary to the parents on how they are raising the child. I recall a family with a child who had a Norwegian mother and an African American father, where the African American grandmother flat out said to her White daughter-in-law, "How is my grandson going to learn to be Black?" This comment was indirectly stating that the way her grandchild is being raised is not acknowledging or honoring his Black heritage. Another example comes from a personal experience I had being involved with a college student group for Filipinx culture more so than the group for my South Asian culture. An Indian student from the South Asian group said to me, "When are you going to participate in our group and do more for your South Asian culture too?"

This policing of performance of identity can take its toll on multiracial individuals. The child can feel overwhelmed by trying to constantly please others or trying to fit in while they are navigating this exploration themselves. Also, succumbing to the opinions of others can place ownership of the definition of identity on others as the authority as to how the culture should be expressed or portrayed by individuals. The other part of this gatekeeping phenomenon that can take its toll on multiracial individuals is that it is laden with judgment. What is this judgment based on? Is it based on some measurement of "purity" of racial identity that the gatekeeper is holding the multiracial individual to? Is it a way of reinforcing to the child the beauty and power of the identity, and not to be ashamed of it? Is it to pass on the essence of the heritage, so it is not diluted or polluted by different forces that pervert the original sense of identity?

The existence of multiracial individuals and how they express identity can be challenging to those around them, because they tend to stretch the definition of what it means to be a part of a certain culture, and expand those boundaries. Even how a person physically looks and is accepted by others can go against what others may see as traditionally a part of the culture, and the child may therefore not be treated as a whole member of the community if the community norms do not accept this expanded notion of identity as a part of the community core. Their allegiances to a certain community may also be challenged if they are skillfully able to **code-switch** and move between cultures. The child and the child's family may be treated as cultural "deviants," and judgment may fall on one or both parents for raising the child in this way.

All of these pressures from external inputs through this "gatekeeper" phenomenon can be taxing on a child and the child's family, and can cause the child and the parents to question their choice of the child's identity, how it is expressed, and the child's ability to fit into the community in question.

Models of Multiracial Identity Development

There has been much scholarly research and exploration regarding how multiracial individuals develop identity. One of the early models on ethnic identity formation[7] explains it in stages an individual goes through, including (1) an *unexamined ethnic identity,* followed by (2) an *ethnic identity search,* and later (3) *ethnic identity achievement.* These traditional theories are useful for conceptualizing monoethnic and monoracial identity development, but they don't always work with multiracial groups. As a result, theories specific to the multiracial experience have been developed.

One foundational theory on biracial identity development[8] emphasizes a stepwise model where an individual (a) has a personal identity not tied to a particular group, then (b) chooses a group, (c) eventually feels a sense of guilt at not being able to express all aspects of their heritage, (d) moves to appreciation of their various racial backgrounds, and (e) finally experiences integration of a multiracial identity. There is pushback on this stepwise model, as an individual may not go through every step, and the idea that struggle is a necessary part of multiracial identity development was not accepted by all.

Indeed, research[9] recognizes that multiracial identity development is not always stepwise but can include advances, repetitions, and retreats. This model based on research with biracial Asians includes interrelated phases that are not linear or mutually exclusive. These include (a) *questioning and confusion,* where an individual feels different and feels a lack of acceptance, (b) *refusal and suppression,* where people attempt to define themselves by choosing one ethnicity over another, (c) *infusion and exploration,* where an embracing of the rejected culture can occur after guilt and other feelings are processed, and (d) *resolution and acceptance,* where there is acknowledgment and equal value of all parts of one's heritage.

Reflection: Do you recognize different patterns in your child's experience of identity; for example, from questioning, being confused, suppression, or exploration and appreciation? These descriptions may be helpful in recognizing the various phases experienced by your child.

Identity can also be understood as subgroups,[10] where multiracial individuals may identify with each heritage community equally (*synthesized integrative identity*), or may prefer one over the other (*functional integrative identity*), where they identify as biracial and adopt both identities (*pluralistic identity*).

Other scholars[11] focus on four categories of biracial identity with Black and White individuals, including a biracial identity (*border identity*), a choice of Black, White, or biracial (*protean identity*), a rejection of racial categorization (*transcendent identity*), and exclusively Black or White (*singular identity*).

Another model[12] asserts that there can be four potentially positive resolutions of biracial identity, including (1) acceptance of the identity society assigns, (2) identification with both racial groups, (3) identification with a single racial group, or (4) identification of a new racial group.

This theory has been developed further through Kristen Renn's research[13] that shows how multiracial individuals may exhibit five patterns of identity:

1. **Monoracial identity:** an individual chooses one of their racial heritages to identify with.

2. **Multiple monoracial identities:** an individual alternates between or among racial heritage group identities. A variety of factors affect which racial heritage group the individual identifies with at a given time or place.

3. **Multiracial identity:** an individual chooses an identity that represents more than one heritage; for example, Mexican and Black.

4. **Extraracial identity:** an individual "opts out" of racial characterization. This pattern may represent a resistance by the individual to categories or social constructions by a dominant, White, monoracial majority.

5. **Situational identity:** an individual moves between or among the above options, and identity can change based upon circumstances and interactions between the individual and their environment.

Discussing Multiracial Identity with Your Child

Using Renn's patterns of multiracial identity as one approach for understanding, here are some questions to consider:

Overall question: What racial identity is your child most comfortable identifying with?

1. Are they choosing one race over the other? (For example, "I identify as fully Sri Lankan.") (*monoracial identity*)

2. Do they choose a different single race at different times? (For example, "I feel more Chinese when I am around my Chinese grandparents; otherwise, I feel and act really White at school.") (*multiple monoracial identities*)

3. Do they find it most authentic to embody a multiracial or biracial heritage? (For example, "I am mixed/multiracial all the time!") (*multiracial identity*)

4. Are they resistant to racial categories and prefer to be "outside the box"? (For example, "I am human.") (*extraracial identity*)

5. Does your child switch between categories, depending upon their circumstances, interactions, or the environment they are in? (For example, "I sometimes feel Pacific Islander around my PI friends, but sometimes feel more Latino when I am at home in my neighborhood, but when I am around my biracial friends at football practice, I definitely like to call myself mixed.") (*situational identity*)

Having terminology to describe the identity pattern that your child is identifying with can be empowering to both you and them. It can help make sense of a child's feelings toward identity, and also help recognize changes that may take place as your child grows; for instance, if your child aligns with one racial heritage over another, or rejects categories overall, or prefers to embody a multiracial identity.

Finally, it is important to remember that racial identity development does not happen in isolation, but occurs within a greater context. Research acknowledging this[14] called the Factor Model of Multiracial Identity (FMMI) incorporates variables such as social and historical context, political awareness and orientation, early experience and socialization, and more. Keeping this in mind, it may be helpful to zoom out and look at what else is going on in a child's world (e.g., changing friend groups, tragic events in the news, or joining a new church) that may affect their identity choice.

ACTIVITY

The following is a self-reflection questionnaire that may be helpful for you in building self-awareness about your own viewpoints toward the identity of the child you are parenting or educating.

As you consider these questions, note which questions are challenging to answer, or those that do not yet have fully formed answers. Also note where you may differ from your partner, family members, or colleagues in your perspectives.

For Parents/Caregivers

1. What race are you choosing to reinforce in your child?

2. What is this choice based on?

3. What biases or blindspots do you have about the racial heritage of your child that is different from your own? Or is the same as your own?

4. Has this conception of identity been communicated to others, including your classroom teacher, religious leaders, fellow community members, neighbors, etc.?

5. How does your partner, or other family or community members, feel about this choice of identity?

6. What biases does your partner, or do your family or community members, have about this or other parts of the child's identity?

7. How will you react if others resist this conception of identity that you have chosen to reinforce in your child?

8. What will you do/how will you react if the child resists this conception of identity, now or later?

9. How will you allow for room for the child to make choices about how they express their identity publicly, especially as they get older?

For Teachers

1. How do you perceive the racial identity of the child in your classroom?

2. Is this in alignment with how the parent identifies the child or how the family sees the child? Or how the child sees themselves?

3. What biases or blindspots do you have about the racial heritage of the child that is different from your own? Or is the same as your own?

4. How will you respond if this conception of identity changes over time?

5. How will you support the child if there are items in the news/current events that involve this part of the child's identity, in either a positive or negative way?

6. Have you asked the parents how they would like the child to be perceived, in terms of the child's racial and cultural identity?

The above questions help cultivate the idea that the raising of a multiracial child involves decisions by the parent when the child is young, and choices by the child when the child gets older. These choices of course are influenced by surrounding factors such as family and community.

Parents may reinforce an identity in the child while they are young; but as the child grows, the child may have a different conception of themselves and choose to identify a different way. Ultimately, the parents can significantly affect the child but cannot force that identity on the child as the child grows older.

It is important to acknowledge how racial identification for multiracial individuals is a continuous layering of experiences, exposure, and reinforcement, and ultimately involves both choice and assignment. This journey of identification also does not exist in a vacuum. Both historical and current events, as well as a community's collective memory of conflict among groups, can deeply impact a child's sense of racial identity and belonging to any particular group.

5

Common and Contemporary Issues

MAGAZINE FEATURES HIGHLIGHT the pulse of what is on the mind of society; and when it comes to race and multiraciality, this has been no exception. The special issue of *Time* magazine on November 18, 1993[1] cover shows a computer-generated face that is a "mix of several races" with the title "The New Face of America," imploring the reading public to react to the growth of migration, and thereby imagine the mixing of different races in the country. When you hover over the image linked to the online back issue,[2] you see credit given to the artist Kin Wah Lam who created the "computer morphing," and a breakdown of races is immediately shared: "Morphed face is 15% Anglo-Saxon, 17.5% Middle Eastern, 17.5% African, 7.5% Asian, 35% Southern European and 7.5% Hispanic." This is such a telling pop-up box, as it shows the fascination of quantifying race in our lives, especially with mixed race people, and how we perceive this visually.

The narrative about imagining multiraciality in society has continued in other publications since then. Using real photographs of multiracial individuals taken by the photographer Martin Schoeller, the October 2013 edition of *National Geographic*[3] invites us to consider the normalcy of mixed race individuals and the idea of a **post-racial** society in the article "The Changing Face of America." These vivid portraits pull the reader in, as we stare at the striking facial features, hair textures, and skin tones that represent a combination of races in juxtaposition with one another. The April 2018 special issue of *National Geographic*[4] shows a cover of biracial twins who phenotypically look different and could be easily labeled as different races by anyone meeting them for the first time. This issue, entitled "Black and White," encourages the reader to look deeply into the foundations of our understanding of race—and to push past these traditional notions.

The usage of imagery of multiracial people is intentionally provoking. The way multiracial individuals are portrayed in these magazines causes us to think about how they are treated in real life. There are a number of different critical issues that arise when thinking through how race is addressed overall, and how multiracial identity is received in particular. We will explore these issues in detail in this chapter as we examine common and contemporary issues that face multiracial youth in school, at home, and in community settings.

What Are You?

The age-old question that multiracial individuals are asked is: "What are you?" This attempt at understanding an individual's race or ethnic background seems to be a rite of passage for multiracial individuals—in that *mostly everyone* experiences it. I have not met a multiracial person who has not been asked this question at one point or another in their life. One Afro-Latina woman shares, "Even though I grew up in Southern California, not a week went by without someone asking me, 'What are you made of?' or 'What are you mixed with?' or 'What's your ethnicity?'" Although ethnic ambiguity can be found within any community or culture, this particular question is the cause of consternation for many multiracial youth, as it points to an "othering" and "objectification" and aim at categorization that the multiracial youth is forced to react to. An individual who identifies as Filipino–Mexican–White shares the struggle with this question: "'What are you?' Constant demanding to know my heritage and then white people especially deciding which I am so they can break my existence down into something remedial they can understand." The experience of being bombarded with this question frequently can have detrimental effects on a person.

How will you teach your child to react to this question? Will this reaction be with humor, active resistance, dismay, or anger—or used as an educational opportunity, a chance to connect, or a time to ignore?

How this question is answered is largely based on the situational context and also the child's feelings in that moment. Perhaps there has been one too many instances of this happening, and the child wishes to no longer engage in this question. Or, in another moment, the child or family members who are present could be in a generous or chatty mood, and answer this with a longer narrative of one's family history. The important thing to note is that there is choice and agency in this matter. A child should not feel obliged to answer this question in any way. Indeed, some youth may create comebacks to this question, like "I'm a girl!" or "I'm human, what are you?" Essentially, this question aims to invite a person to define themselves to the person who is curious about the answer. Similarly, the question "Where are you from?" may be a way that the questioner is trying to share their curiosity about your child's culture, race, or ethnicity.

Microaggressions

The "What are you?" and "Where are you from?" questions are examples of subtle insults known as microaggressions. Racial microaggressions are defined by scholar Dr. D. W. Sue[5] as "brief and commonplace and daily verbal, behavioral, and environmental indignities, whether intentional or unintentional, that communicate hostile, derogatory, or negative" messages to racially marginalized groups within society. An example of a racial microaggression was shared with me by a neighbor whose biracial Black and White eleven-year-old daughter was told by her White peers that her hair looks better when it's straight than when it's curly. This commentary can reinforce in the girl that being White is more favorable than being Black. As of now, she herself has adopted a preference for straight hair. Her parents are supportive of her hairstyle choices but are also questioning if this is impacting her affinity with her African American heritage and biracial identity overall. As we can see, the consequences of racial microaggressions can go beyond the moment itself and can compound into larger, longer-term challenges to self-esteem, racial identity formation, and feelings of belonging.

Other scholars have described racial microaggressions[6] as "a form of everyday, systemic racism that upholds the status quo, specifically white supremacy." As we can see from this biracial child's example with hairstyle preference, the superiority of Whiteness is reinforced by her friends—whether it is done knowingly or unknowingly. Although White supremacy impacts the experience of many multiracial children and directly affects racially minoritized groups, it is also important to expand this understanding of racial oppression through microaggressions to include actions *by* monoracial groups of color, in upholding each group's *own* monoracial status quo.

An example of this type of racial microaggression happened with my sister (who phenotypically looks more Filipina than myself) as a youth, when she arrived at a South Asian community gathering separately from the rest of our family, and a greeter asked her if she was in the right place or needed directions to somewhere else. This imparted the message that she didn't belong at the event, nor in the community overall—solely based on her appearance. This kind of reaction can happen in monoracial communities where the general population may not have contact with or exposure to multiethnic, multiracial, or transracially adopted individuals. There is a limited worldview and understanding of who can and does belong within a given group. Again, the microaggression occurs in order to uphold the status quo as it is seen and perceived. As we can see, there are lived experiences of multiracial individuals that go beyond the dichotomy of White supremacy and pro-Blackness. Within the dominating narratives of White privilege and anti-Blackness, there exists a spectrum of experience among multiracial individuals that is often not talked about, yet it is so complex and present in our multiracial children's lives. In her TED Talk,[7] the Nigerian novelist Chimamanda Ngozi Adichie reminds us of "the danger of a single story" in thinking that experiences are ubiquitous, for this is not the case.

What is extremely important in looking at the "What are you?" question, and with any microaggression, is the push and pull dynamic of **intent versus impact.** This refers to ascertaining the intent of the person asking the question, and acknowledging the impact that it has on the recipient. If the intention of the interaction is positive, perhaps knowledge of that can be motivating for an individual to take up the conversation further. However, if it is meant with the aim to hurt, tease, or cause harm, that will call for a different reaction and the possible need for defense. An important point to note is that even if the intentions of the person asking the question were to positively further the dialogue, or if the intent itself is undetermined, a child can still be hurt in the interaction. Indeed, good intentions are not enough to excuse the negative outcome in the situation, i.e., "I didn't mean it in a bad way—you shouldn't take it badly" or "You are too sensitive." It is important in that moment for the adult to honor a child's feelings and to encourage the child to acknowledge their reactions as valid, meaningful, and important. It is also critical for the child to do the same for themselves, especially when discomfort or emotional harm is ignited by the situation. We must recognize the impact an interaction has on an individual and realize that the intention behind an utterance or a behavior doesn't excuse its negative consequences.

Multiracial Microaggressions

Academic scholars Dr. Marc Johnston-Guerrero (formerly Johnston) and Dr. Kevin Nadal have outlined the common microaggressions[8] that are specific to the multiracial and multiethnic person's experience and how one can be impacted by **monoracism**.[9] This groundbreaking work, based partly on Maria P. P. Root's original research, forms a "taxonomy" of **multiracial microaggressions** that is incredibly helpful in thinking about how to prepare children and youth who will likely face a form of this at some point in their lives. The "What are you?" question is a common example of a multiracial microaggression. Multiracial microaggressions can occur in a number of ways and also relay deeply impactful messages that youth may internalize as a result of being exposed to these sentiments. These overarching themes stated by Johnston and Nadal include exclusion and isolation; exoticization and objectification; assumption of a monoracial identity; denial of a multiracial identity; and pathologizing of multiracial identity and experiences.

Exclusion and Isolation

This can occur when a child is challenged for attempting to live out or claim a multiracial identity, rather than a singular monoracial identity. It can also take place when family or community members exclude multiracial individuals from actively feeling a sense of belonging within the group or in a given interaction. The resulting message is that the child is not worthy of being recognized or included, and that their recognition of multiple heritages is neither valid nor valued.

Examples:

- An uncle will not interact with his biracial nephews in the same way that he interacts with his monoracial nephews; he treats his monoracial relatives with more familiarity, affinity, and understanding than his multiracial ones.

- A child is not invited to perform a traditional dance for a Native American community festival, because they have White heritage and it is assumed they don't know the music or the movements or wouldn't be interested in performing.

- A person identifying as White, East Asian, and Southeast Asian explains: "I had a lot of issues feeling a sense of connection and belonging. Though mixed race, I went to an all-white school where kids would make fun of me by squinting to replicate 'Asian eyes' and where even teachers would ask me where I'm 'really from' when I told them I was born in Europe. On the other hand, my Asian family would often tell me to my face that they viewed me as white."

- A White and Pakistani individual shares that "as a kid I was always on display to perform: 'Can you say this in Urdu?'"

Exoticization and Objectification

Individuals who are multiracial may be noticed for their outward appearance and be treated in an idealized way. This is evidenced by statements like "You have good genes because you are mixed" or "Blended babies are beautiful." Although these comments may seem like compliments, they overlook an individual's sense of self, and instead objectify them in a way that can make them feel less of a person. This may also make the youth feel abnormal and on display.

Example:

☙ Asian teenage girls are putting on makeup, getting ready for a party, and a multiracial girl's friend says to her, "Your makeup looks better on you than me because you're mixed" as a comment on her facial features being superior to monoracial Asian facial features.

☙ A Chinese and White American woman shares, "I was told half Asian girls were hot, because they get Asian skinniness, small nose, tan skin."

☙ A Filipina–Irish American woman describes, "I didn't feel 'otherized' until later in high school when I went to overnight camp. A girl at camp found out I was half Filipina and would go on and on about how she loved Filipino people because they were so cute and adorable. I didn't understand why this felt awkward and uncomfortable while it was happening. But when I went home and had time to think about it, I figured out how the exotification made me feel otherized."

Assumption of a Monoracial Identity

A lack of nuanced understanding and assumptions about a multiracial individual's identity or family dynamics can commonly be experienced. The assumption is that a parent or family member is not related to the child, because the phenotype does not exactly match. Or that everyone in a group is monoracial and doesn't hold multiple identities at the same time, so it is acceptable to make comments or slurs about other groups (which may be a group that the multiracial person actually also belongs to).

Examples:

☙ A school counselor automatically signs a child up for an **affinity group** on campus, based on the child's name and physical appearance, without asking the child if they identify with that group or feel comfortable participating.

🐦 A Latina mother who picks up her lighter-skinned biracial child is mistaken for a nanny by the staff and is asked for her ID and if the family has given her permission to pick up the toddler from the daycare.

🐦 A joke is made about "red Indians" in front of a biracial Native American youth, because his White friends weren't aware of or didn't remember his Indigenous heritage.

🐦 A Liberian–Asian person tells a story: "Just recently, I went to get fingerprinted for a new job. The woman started to fill out the application and when she got to the race part, she immediately chose Black. It feels so incomplete to just have one of the two racial groups I am a part of listed on file. I don't have any issues with identifying as Black (I'm very proud of it), but I find that my Asian side is ignored a great deal of the time."

🐦 A Filipino–Polish–Irish–French Canadian individual shares, "My biggest challenge was answering the question 'Where are you from?' And 'What are you?' Whatever I answered was most often met with 'You don't look Asian, are you sure?' Or 'You look too white to be multiracial.' It usually was meant to be a compliment."

🐦 A Japanese, American, and Dutch individual expresses, "To be a child and be exoticized by adults because you are mixed race and have such 'pretty lips' is truly not okay. You begin to learn that your body is not your own, but rather at the mercy of how White or Asian your skin, your hair, your eyes, your lips are as defined by adults."

Denial of a Multiracial Identity

This occurs when a child is not allowed or encouraged to choose a multiracial identity. This can readily happen when a child is in a dominant, majority-race group and made to feel that they have to heavily perform the dominant identity in order to fit in and be accepted, or cannot choose a multiracial identity.

Examples:

- A biracial child is told they sound too much like a "White person" when they are around their Black friends and are teased and ridiculed for their choice of language.

- A biracial Asian youth feels peer pressure in bringing their non-Asian boyfriend to a gathering that is mostly people with an Asian background, and is met with stares when they arrive.

- A powerful example of this comes from a woman who identifies as Filipino/Chicano (Mexican American, Irish, British, and Scottish):

> *Once I became a mother my daughter ended up taking after her father and is dark skinned with dark brown hair. When she was in kindergarten they had an art assignment where they were supposed to draw how they see themselves and she drew herself with light skin, blond hair, and blue eyes. It really hurt me to see that my baby didn't see herself as beautiful, she couldn't be beautiful unless she was white, and it was my fault because I was always putting my white heritage first and my Filipino and Chicano heritage last.*

- Another heart-wrenching account comes from a person who identifies as Ethiopian (Black) and Chinese, and who grew up in Asia until she was eight years old:

> *... because everyone around had beautiful long, straight, black locks, I was jealous. This jealousy led to hating more than just my hair;*

I hated having dark skin, I hated having a "big nose," I hated having a long face and pointy chin—I hated being Black. Hearing comments like "She is actually really beautiful, just a bit too Black" from complete strangers became a self-esteem destruction. I was jealous of others for being one race, and I wanted to just be Asian because that was the environment that I was brought up in.

Pathologizing of Multiracial Identity and Experiences

This occurs when a multiracial person's identity or experiences are seen as troubled and are viewed as psychologically abnormal.

Examples:

- The assumption is made that a multiracial child's parents are divorced, because of the inaccurate conclusion that interracial relationships have many problems.

- A child's behavioral issues at school are thought to be a result of their multiracial identity and interracial family dynamics, and are pitied: "It's because they are in a mixed-up family."

These multiracial microaggressions are actually signs of deeper issues regarding race relations that exist in many countries.

News items show how these microaggressions extend into deeper societal views of multiraciality.

One example comes from 2009[10] when a Louisiana court justice would not marry a Black and White couple out of concern for their potentially bringing a biracial child into the world. He underscores how he is not racist toward any particular group: "I do ceremonies for black couples right here in my house." He states his "main concern is for the children" and has come to the conclusion, after having "discussed the topic with blacks and whites, along with witnessing some interracial marriages," that "most of black society does not readily accept offspring of such relationships, and neither does white society." He goes on to say that he doesn't "do interracial marriages because I don't want to put children in a situation they didn't bring on themselves," furthering the point by sharing, "In my heart, I feel the children will later suffer." Here we see how the positive *intentions* of this person (i.e., preventing harm and discomfort for a child who is the product of an interracial union) cause the negative *impact* of harm, distress, and even inequity in this case.

As was mentioned, individuals may not use the term "mixed" or "mixed race" because it triggers the negative, pathologizing conception that being multiracial means you are "mixed up." This connects back to this judgment about how being "mixed" is a struggle and an issue.

As we have discussed in other chapters, there is a lack of acceptance of the fluidity of identity, and therefore the living out of an identity in a multilayered way.

A Framework for Teaching about and Responding to Microaggressions

Activities for Young Children: Teaching about Microaggressions

Mosquito Bites

Explaining microaggressions to young children can be done! I heard a colleague explain it to me using this analogy:

> *Microaggressions are like mosquito bites. One tiny bite hurts a little bit and you might ignore it, but it can still itch and bother you. And a lot of mosquito bites are really uncomfortable and annoying!*

Encourage children to pay attention to words or situations, even if they want to brush it off as "just a little thing." Listen to your child when they share a microaggression instance with you, and model that it is important that it is acknowledged and addressed.

Ouch! Moments

A wonderful book that can introduce this topic is called *Ouch! Moments: When Words Are Used in Hurtful Ways* by Michael Genhart.[11] Read this book with your child and have a discussion about words they have heard or said that are hurtful, and how to deal with situations when that happens. This book includes a fantastic note to parents and caregivers by Dr. Kevin L. Nadal that includes tips for talking to children when they are both the target and the enactor of microaggressions. The story starts off with a child experiencing a bee sting—another example that a child can understand, and that can connect back to the mosquito analogy.

Responding to Microaggressions: A Framework for Reaction

In working with many multiracial children and families, I have noticed a pattern of how the "What are you?" question and other multiracial microaggressions can be answered in the moment toward a potential outcome. Based on examples shared with me over the years, I have created a framework for addressing microaggressions that was first mentioned in the illustrated handbook *Being All of Me*[12] created in partnership with the Multiracial Americans of Southern California (MASC), a longstanding nonprofit organization committed to social and educational support and advocacy for multiracial families. This framework has the acronym CHATS and can be utilized by parents, caregivers, and educators in an effort to teach all children how they can react to potentially challenging conversations that they will likely be met with in regards to race.

🍂 **Counter:** Counter the commentary through direct resistance and reaction.

A dear friend who identifies as African American and Tamil Sri Lankan shares, "When interacting with African Americans who may ask what I'm mixed with, I am often replied to by them with a 'Whatever—you're Black.' They may laugh, they may be serious. I can laugh with them or just shrug at their response. But I continue to assert that I am Black *and* something else. Over years of doing this, all of my social circle knows I am a Black woman who is *also* Sri Lankan."

🍂 **Hide:** Withdraw from the conversation. This is a purposeful choice; it is not seen as a weakness. It can be used especially in unsafe or troubling situations.

An example from a Filipino White (Irish and Italian) individual: "I sometimes get mistaken for other ethnicities or races. One of the more upsetting incidents was at the local library, when a stranger asked if I spoke Spanish. I denied it (because I can't), and he instantly got angry, accusing me of lying: 'I know you do.' As it was a library, I was able to de-escalate the situation by backing away and moving to another aisle." This is an example of how withdrawing from a situation can be an effective method to avoid further harm. This individual shared, "The result was likely just someone assuming I was a liar and ashamed of my heritage," so it is important for a parent or caregiver to debrief this incident with the child, reinforcing how this is a powerful choice and the right thing to do in that moment.

🍂 **Ask for Help / Seek Allies:** Seek assistance with the situation from others, either an authority figure, a peer, or another individual.

Example from a multiracial (African American, Irish, Eastern European, and Jewish) parent of a multiracial child: "I have had the experience of being mistaken for my children's nanny. There is an employee at my child's school who clearly cannot get her head around the fact that I'm the mom of this blond-haired, light-eyed child. The first time she saw me at pickup she tried to challenge me; thankfully another teacher who knew me 'vouched' for me before it escalated. Now whenever she sees me with my kid she just stares at me like she's still trying to figure it out." This is an example of an ally who could step in and address the microaggression in the moment.

- **Teachable Moment:** Respond to the situation as a teachable moment, taking the time and making an effort to inform the other person of a different perspective.

A biracial Black and White person describes, "In high school and college, I decided to identify as a biracial person, not as a black person who happened to have a white mom. I felt like it was an unpopular choice, but to be otherwise was not authentic." Responding to situations to inform people about all aspects of a person's multiracial identity is utilizing it as a teachable moment for others.

- **Similarities:** Find similarities with other examples to bring about learning for the other individual.

An example of furthering a teachable moment through similarities comes from a person who is Filipino and Mexican:

When I was in LA for the first Filipino Food Festival, there was a couple in front of me; the husband was white and the wife was Filipino. We started talking about how we heard about the event and if we had ever had Filipino food. When I told the couple I was Filipino and that I had been eating Filipino food my entire life, the husband looked at me and said, 'But you're not full, right?' I looked down and said, 'No, my father is Mexican.' He started laughing and responded, 'Ah, that makes more sense. With the way you look, I thought there is no way she could be full Filipino.' I started to explain how there were many cultural similarities between Filipinos and Mexicans due to a shared colonial past.

We must not ignore that situations like these described can definitely be challenging. This person who shared the example from the food festival shares further, "I was really angry and upset that this white man was trying to tell me that I wasn't Filipino, when I know I am. Questioning my identity has been difficult, but it has become a normal part of living this way."

Given how challenging situations can be, it is important when teaching this framework to point out that the child or other family member has a sense of agency in that they are able to choose how to react to the situation. By showing them how they have the power of choice, it is very empowering as it allows the child to take ownership of the situation, rather than feel they are passively experiencing the event as a victim or a bystander. Having discussions about how to deal with difficult scenarios creates resilience in children as well as develops a skill-set that they are able to incorporate into real-life situations as they encounter curiosity about, resistance to, and challenge to their racial identities. This is essential to highlight in any dialogue with children about when they face uncomfortable encounters that evoke a variety of feelings within them and those around them.

Special Topics in Multiracial Identity: Family

Siblings and Other Family Members

As we saw in the example of the *National Geographic* issue featuring the biracial Black and White twins who looked vastly different from one another, siblings from the same family may have differing physical appearances and may be treated differently as a result. The preference for lighter skin in many communities, known as colorism, can cause a darker-skinned child to encounter more unconscious bias, and a lighter-skinned child to have more privileges in certain aspects of society. In communities of color, there may be a preference for darker skin over lighter skin, as a pushback to general mainstream colorism, and a multiracial child may be perceived and judged to be receiving unearned privileges due to their lighter skin. The experience of colorism of a multiracial person within a community of color or in general society can vary greatly based on the friend circles the child is a part of, and how able they are to articulate and hold their racial identity position within these environments. Consequently, a multiracial individual's worldview may be completely different from that of a sibling or other close family member with the same racial background due to their experiences in society. One child may resent an aspect of their identity or be excluded for it (e.g., hair type, skin color, or language use), whereas a sibling or cousin with the same background may highlight it and be celebrated for it. These experiences can happen in the same family, *at the same time.* Also, a child's experience and conception of their racial identity can change over time, so this experience of and preference for identity is not static.

A parent, caregiver, or educator must be ready to acknowledge the potential differences between siblings and other close family members, and especially between the child and adults in the family.

The safest and most comprehensive ways to support a child are to not assume that their experience and conception of racial identity are the same as that of a sibling or other close family member; and to continue to have open and positive dialogue regarding the journey of identity that the child is on. The way to promote a healthy sense of self is to be accepting of the child, whatever stage they are in with their experience of identity, and to understand the complexity of how that experience can be different from that of other family members.

An example of this is if a coach has a student on their sports team and notices that the racial backgrounds of the friend group of one child are different from those of a younger sibling who they coach in a subsequent year—to not point it out or make them feel belittled or abnormal because of that difference.

Family jokes can be meant as fun in passing but can be detrimental to a child's self-esteem overall. I witnessed a vivid example of this when a biracial lighter-skinned White and Iranian young adult brought his White Bulgarian partner to a family dinner, and his younger darker-skinned brother brought his Indian partner. At the gathering, the young man's Iranian aunt made a joke in front of both siblings and their partners that "one of you likes White, and the other one likes Brown!" The awkward exchange highlighted the differences between the brothers and reinforced how vastly different their worldviews and choices could be, widening a gap in their relationship that already existed due to how they are treated by society. This also, in turn, communicated to their partners and everyone at the dinner that the differences are to be made fun of, and the partners also felt objectified as a consequence of this attempt at humor.

As parents, caregivers, and educators of multiracial children, we must recognize the different experiences that siblings and close family members may have. We should make an effort to be mindful of assumptions and language that characterize the understanding that siblings from the same multiracial family may look the same, feel the same, and experience the same things, even though this is often not the case. This assumption of similarity is another micro-aggression that children face at home, at school, and in the community, related to this particular topic of family differences.

Family Dynamics

Families come in all different forms. It is important to recognize that a child's exposure to their culture and elements associated with their race can be more or less pronounced depending upon the family setting that the child is raised in. In my research on multiethnic Filipinx young adults,[13] I found that youth who were in families that had a single parent or who were more exposed to a certain culture had more affinity for the racial identity of the parent they were raised with, due to family communication patterns in the home environment, amplified by what opinions surround them in society.

One example shared by a Filipino–German individual demonstrates this phenomenon:

I kinda felt German as a kid, until my dad passed away and I was only left with my mother. I noticed that German/white people looked at me differently without a German parent. Now I was an immigrant kid, not a German kid to them. I started to feel ashamed about my Filipino roots, my brown skin, the accent of my mother. I really wanted to be white. It took me years to change my mind.

Another example from a multiracial Japanese and Mexican woman shows how this can occur:

My Japanese mother would criticize the features that came from my Mexican dad, sparking some insane internal racism, self-hate, and abysmal self-esteem growing up. I was always too dark,

not petite enough, and my hair was a "bird's
nest" (it's just curly). On top of that, I was never
really exposed to my dad's culture because he
was always working. For the longest time I hated
being half Mexican and tried to distance
myself from it as much as I could. The more I
learned about the mixed experience and about
Mexican culture, the less inner turmoil I felt.

In contrast, a child who is in close contact with both sides of
their extended family could have a positive sense of each of their
identities and pride about their culture and heritage as a multiracial person, at the same time. This lived experience is due to the
reinforcement of identity through the family environment and is
particularly pronounced by the family dynamics that the child is
raised in.

Parents, caregivers, and educators should be mindful of the
varying degrees of contact, familiarity, loyalty, understanding, and
pride that a child can internalize and espouse as a result of their
family upbringing.

Intersectionality and Multidimensionality

Developed by Black feminist theorists and coined by Kimberlé
Crenshaw,[14] intersectionality refers to the intersecting aspects of
identity that can compound to influence one's identity, thereby
impacting one's experience of both privilege and marginalization.
It can be described as the "many axes that work together and influence each other."[15] This is important to understand with respect to
multiracial identity, because it is already complex, and what this
means is that it doesn't exist in a vacuum. Someone who is multiracial and is an immigrant with a native language other than English
can have a vastly different experience than a mixed race person born
and raised in the United States. Or a multiracial person who is

queer identifying may experience a pronounced sense of oppression, more so than monoracial counterparts who identify as cisgender and heterosexual. This lens of intersectionality brings forth a lens of deeper understanding and empathy toward a person's given situation.

Multidimensionality acknowledges the intersectionality among social phenomena such as racism and sexism. These systemic experiences don't exist in a singular way and in fact are intersecting, and are not experienced the same way by everyone. This idea of multidimensionality acknowledges how a multiracial person can experience privilege, oppression, and other phenomena in many ways, or ways different from others.

These terms work hand in hand to acknowledge the complexity and intersection of both identity and the societal forces we are exposed to.[16]

Dating, Friendships, and Other Relationships

Youth can find dating and forming relationships to be a challenge when they are encountering potential friends, potential partners, or the families of friends and partners who are not as aware of or accepting of multiracial identity. There can also be bias and assumptions about a person's phenotype when participating in dating apps or interacting online with others.

A multiracial Asian and Latinx youth shared with me that although he looks phenotypically Latinx, he is interested in dating Asian men, who "will not give him the time of day" because of their preference for monoracial Asian men. Despite sending them family photos that showed that he in fact had an Asian parent, there was a sense of exclusion and a lack of acceptance for his multiracial identity.

How to support a child who is navigating these dynamics and challenges? It is important to maintain open lines of communication and be a sounding board for when difficulties arise. Also, exposing children to families who are accepting and celebratory of differences and multiracial families can be extremely fulfilling for the child.

Adoption and Transracial Adoption

Families with adopted children may face additional challenges of the complexities of cultivating a sense of belonging for the child. Families with transracial adoptees have some similarities with multiracial families in that the parent's and the child's racial identity may be different from one another, or there may be differences in appearance that can cause questioning by others. The transracial adoptee may also be multiracial and have the additional opportunity to explore more than one racial or cultural heritage. It is important to consider the experiences of children who are a part of an adoptee family. How is race being taught to them? How does the greater, extended family react to or reinforce their identity? There are similar issues between transracial adoptees and multiracial children around purposefully supporting a child's racial identity, and also some very unique aspects that are different between these groups.

Multifaith Families

Multiracial families of differing spiritual and religious backgrounds have the added complexity and intersectionality of potentially needing to address racial and religious bias that can occur within family dynamics. Parents of differing religious affiliations may be challenged in deciding what faith to raise their child in, particularly if their religious institutions have congregations heavily from a certain race that may not be as familiar with interracial unions and multiracial children. Years ago, I facilitated a workshop at the Skirball Cultural Center in Los Angeles with psychologist and author Dr. Joel Crohn on how to have successful intercultural relationships. Within that workshop, there were numerous attendees who highlighted how raising multiracial children in addition to their interreligious union was a challenge. Interracial couples shared their experiences of how certain congregations with a dominant racial group were less accepting of partners and family members who were racially different from the majority. Even though spirituality can be a unifying force, it is not free from the bias that humans harbor regarding racial differences.

DNA Ancestry Testing

DNA testing for ethnicity and genealogy is now widely available and has been marketed as a way to connect with one's culture, ethnic heritage, and family members. Although this can be appealing to those who wish to explore their ancestry further—including multiracial individuals—one should take heed of potential issues. First, there are privacy concerns, as the data is sold to other companies for use in research such as drug development, and anonymity may be compromised as this data is passed on to other providers.

Second, there is scrutiny[17] around the accuracy of test results, since there can be different results for the same person, depending upon the database used, and the genetic markers used to come up with the results. Also, the DNA data used to generate the results is only a portion of the genome, so it can heavily skew the outcome. Companies that sell these services "don't share their data, and their methods are not validated by an independent group of scientists and there are not agreed-upon standards of accuracy."

At a conference panel presentation, transracial adoptee and scholar Dr. Aeriel Ashlee[18] shared how her first DNA test revealed that she was Korean plus other Asian ethnicities, only to do the test later with results stating that she was indeed only of Korean ancestry. Ashlee described what an emotional rollercoaster it was for her to experience this changing information, as it had huge implications for her identity as a transracial adoptee who was going through the process of exploration of the meaning of her own identity.

Another consideration with DNA testing is the potential of finding out about family members that you did not know about before. For many people, this is an exciting and joyous opportunity to connect with newfound relatives! However, that outcome can also be challenging. A student affairs coordinator who is multiracial shared with me that her mixed race husband took a DNA test and found out that he had a half-brother that he previously knew nothing about. It completely changed and somewhat disrupted their lives as he yearned to connect further with his brother and also learn more about the culture and heritage that they shared. The attention to this new relative created a challenging dynamic within his immediate and extended family, compounded by the effects of navigating race, as both siblings were multiracial BIPOC individuals, but of different racial backgrounds.

Although DNA testing can be a helpful tool to connect with other family members and to learn more about one's ethnic background, there are some aspects of it that can be seen as a concern. An issue related to the topic of multiracial identity is how DNA testing can undermine one's sense of identity if there is a lower percentage of a certain racial composition than a person thought, or if suddenly knowing about a new ethnic heritage is enough of a connection to an ethnic or racial identity for a person to feel comfortable claiming it. These larger questions about "proving" oneself as a multiracial person are amplified with the rise of DNA testing.

All of the issues shared in this chapter require further reflection, dialogue, and processing with your child. Although the answers or suggested actions to these complex scenarios may not be clear, knowing that these situations exist and may be ones that you encounter can help you prepare for when that moment does arise.

For more in-depth discussion on common issues faced by multiracial children, please refer to the parenting and teaching resources listed in chapter 9, including the following resources: *Raising Mixed Race: Multiracial Asian Children in a Post-Racial World* by Sharon H. Chang, *Meeting the Needs of Multiethnic and Multiracial Children in Schools* by Dr. Francis Wardle and Marta I. Cruz-Janzen, *Does Anybody Else Look Like Me? A Parent's Guide to Raising Multiracial Children* by Donna Jackson Nakazawa, *Multiracial Child Resource Book: Living Complex Identities* edited by Maria P. P. Root and Matt Kelley, and *Multiracial Cultural Attunement* by Kelly Faye Jackson and Gina Miranda Samuels.

6

Teaching Racial/Multiracial Identity in the Classroom

THERE IS A MEMORY that is seared into my mind—the moment when race and skin color were first brought to my attention as a young girl. I was in grade one in an elementary school in Vancouver, Canada, and was assigned a grade seven buddy who happened to be White. We met throughout the year, doing joint activities together. One of the activities was to draw a portrait of our buddy, and share them with each other. I can never forget the moment my grade seven buddy shared her depiction of me—she had used a peach-colored crayon, which all the kids in my class, and even I, referred to as the "skin color crayon." My buddy took a second look at her drawing and loudly pronounced, "Oh, your skin is not *that* color!" and she then took a brown crayon out of the box and scribbled all over the picture of my face. It actually didn't match my skin but looked like a big, muddy mess to me—and felt as if my face was a big error that needed to be scrawled over. Being this young and having never had a discussion about race in my life,

I didn't say anything; I just watched it happen. To this day, I still have never shared this story with my parents or even my sibling and can't erase this indelible image and feeling of being othered from my memories of being a child.

As we have already explored, there is much evidence that children recognize race at a young age. The next question is: what do they think about it? And how can we mold and sculpt that learning about racial differences in a positive direction? If we are not intentional in what we are impressing upon our children, societal messages can influence how young people see race. A number of years ago, Anderson Cooper re-created a study done by researchers on the perception of skin color among children and captured the results on video.[1] He and the researchers separately asked children to point at which skin color picture the children thought was good or bad, which ones they would like to be, and which one adults favor. Most children demonstrated a bias, even at an incredibly young age. There were some children who demonstrated that inclusive notions of equity prevailed. In each case, it makes us wonder: what can we as adults do to teach a sense of equity among racial skin color and different racially lived experiences, and to offset messages of bias that our children could be exposed to?

In professional development trainings, I often share with parents, caregivers, teachers, and support staff a plethora of supplies and resources that can help surface and further the conversation about race, identity, and culture within the home or the classroom. My absolute favorite are multicultural crayons, or People Colors crayons, that come in a variety of shades that truly look like the variety of skin tones that are present in the world! These supplies also come in the form of markers, colored pencils, and construction paper. Materials such as these are a vital component of a child being able to choose the representation of themselves that is accurate, thereby developing comfort and pride in how they see themselves in the world; and push past norms of Whiteness as the default skin color that is so prominent on TV, in films, in magazines, and in other information sources that we commonly consume. Whiteness as the "default color" of people is so widespread, we have to actively counter against it with the toys, books, and supplies we choose to have in our home and in the classroom. This is incredibly important when supporting the identity development of a multiracial child who may not have a family member or friend with the exact same identity or physical appearance as they have. So, it is important to support the understanding that a range of racial identities and physical appearances can exist within a child's life. Chapter 9 lists some of my top resources for actively approaching race and skin color at home or in the classroom.

In my own home, I shared a set of People Colors crayons with my oldest son when he was six years old and encouraged him to use a variety of skin tones when he drew pictures of people and did his take-home projects. We practiced matching the skin tone of me, his younger brother, his father, and other people in our family, since we all happen to be different shades. I even asked questions about which crayon matched other people in his class, sports figures, or other people he has seen on TV or in books. At one point, I went as far as to make it mandatory for him to show a variety of skin tones in his homework illustrations—or I wouldn't deem it complete and he couldn't go on to play! We worked on these concepts for weeks. Of course, like any parent, I questioned myself and wondered, "Is this really making a difference?" and "Am I overdoing it with the race thing?" At one point, I eased up but left the crayons within easy reach so he could choose to use them himself. One day, about a month later, I finally had affirmation of the impact of these efforts when I came across a piece of homework he completed without me, and I saw that he colored all of the people in the picture with both dark and light skin tones. There was normalcy about the fact that there was variety in his understanding of race and skin color—and he willingly chose to represent that, on his own. The concept of a single "skin color crayon" that I had grown up with was defeated. Hurray!

During graduate school at the University of Hawai'i at Mānoa was the first time I became acquainted with materials and also methods that support multicultural learning in the classroom. I took a graduate-level multicultural education class from Dr. Patricia E. Halagao, an ardent Filipina activist, educator, professor, and role model who specializes in critical multicultural education. I learned about how to honor history and truth that isn't in textbooks, examine systemic inequity that exists in education, as well as initiate perspective-taking that is essential to building deep understanding and empathy for a variety of groups other than our own. From that point, I went on to be a part of a curriculum design project team led by Dr. Halagao for the Smithsonian Institution, creating an online curriculum on Filipino American History, in commemoration of the centennial of when Filipinos first arrived in the United States, which included key information that is not readily found in any mainstream textbook, except for a curriculum she herself had co-authored called "Pinoy Teach." I witnessed firsthand how our recognition of history, culture, and identity impacted Filipinx students and students from other cultural backgrounds to understand concepts like revolution and **colonialism** from the perspective of those who had been colonized or who had migrated to work on plantations.

The biggest takeaway for me from this period is how we as educators are in fact revolutionaries who mirror those in our own history. Resisting the dominant frameworks is a battle in itself. This involves challenging the status quo of what we are taught in traditional educational paradigms and insisting that the curriculum we uphold includes a fuller conception of history and reality where we can see ourselves and our ancestors. This "decolonization of our minds" and lives begins with each of us learning and sharing fuller, deeper knowledge with others, and providing the opportunity to access it without the same struggle and bias we experienced in our own educational careers. As these messages are elevated, we must support those who not only have undergone trauma from the loss of connection to history and culture, but are retraumatized as they become aware of that tragic loss. That is why any lasting impact around educational and racial equity must involve some component of healing.*

Dr. Halagao's teachings, my additional coursework on ethnic studies, and this Smithsonian project combined to be an instrumental thrust that pushed me to reevaluate my approach to education, including what I was originally taught as an educator in my formative years. Although I am a credentialed teacher, during my entire teacher education program, there was not one course that adequately talked about the needs of multicultural classrooms or looked at race, identity, and culture as a part of the pedagogy in a way that we could take and practically implement into the classroom. How could this be the case?

As I talk and work with more and more teachers and schools in my consulting work, I can see there is a gap around awareness, skills, and methods to really bring the conversation about race and identity into the classroom in an effective way. It would be inaccurate to put the blame squarely on individuals, as if the lack of preparation or understanding is entirely their fault. Teacher education programs also have to include noteworthy efforts toward advancing the conversation about race, inclusion, and identity. The training, dialogue, and practice are essential so teachers can feel equipped to address this appropriately in the classroom. We don't always have that in the circles of professional development that

---

* Restorative justice and other processes that center a deeper human and community connection and involve healing among children and adults are a step forward in this direction. For more tools and discussion around this, please visit World Trust Educational Services and the work of Dr. Shakti Butler at www.world-trust.org.

educators are exposed to, but it is indeed crucial. Not only is it a sensitive subject—and one that is perceived to be a minefield from the viewpoint of many—but there is pressure to do an adequate job in order to build the most effective outcomes for students. The risks are high. Lessons and units have to be in alignment with official curriculum standards, there must be support from administration to be able to broach this topic, and also—how will parents react? This is a lot to manage. However, the biggest possible risk we must acknowledge is leaving our children unprepared or their potential unrealized. This should motivate us to take action.

I recall teaching a very successful institution-wide professional development program on inclusion, equity, and diversity at a local elementary school. We tied the program into the citizenship principles already in place at the school about respect and belonging. I conducted student assemblies on these topics with children of all ages, discussing microaggressions that children may not realize they are partaking in. This was all shared in child-friendly language appropriate for their age levels. We discussed how to be advocates for inclusion and "interrupters" of bias and othering, rather than be complicit with peer pressure and exclusion. Children approached me that day, and even weeks later, to express how our session together helped show how we can attend to differences in a positive way, and helped foster an environment of inclusion and respect.

Despite these successes, when children went home and shared what they learned that day, some parents misinterpreted the intention of the program as "bringing too much attention to differences," and they then called the principal to share concerns—some even complained. Fortunately, the principal and the overall school administration I was working with were 100% supportive and helped to address the parents' concerns, and explain both the purpose of and the methods behind the program.

This example calls into question how we can present the importance of learning about race, identity, and inclusion to the overall school community—from parents to children to teaching faculty and support staff—as an integral part of the curriculum that is supportive of children's overall growth. It is important to acknowledge how this is a multipronged effort, involving alignment among the school, individual teachers, as well as the home with caregivers and parents. This comprehensive approach is in contrast to being reactive to images of racial unrest in the media or misunderstandings that will inevitably occur in the classroom—which, in this current societal climate, seems like a ticking time bomb waiting to explode. We *cannot* wait for a racial incident to occur in a child's life, or disparaging news items about race to hurt our children, for us to move into action to talk about race. I have seen schools make a concerted effort only after multiple racial incidents have occurred, and it is demoralizing for all involved to have to deal with difficult conversations and actions after the damage is already done. This work must be done *proactively* in an overall institutional effort, with teachers, parents, caregivers, school administrators, and support staff all in alignment about the value of the content and the process at hand.

So how can this be done? What is the blueprint for proactively cultivating conversations and incorporating activities about racial understanding into the education and overall development of our children? In this chapter and in Appendix C, I outline sample key activities that can be shared to start the conversation about race, and also a flow of the lesson that incorporates learning and exploration about multiracial identity. It is important to adapt these activities to the audience you are serving, and to make sure they are adequate for the developmental level of the children. To this end, I have suggested age brackets where certain activities may be more appropriate and effective. This is a partial list, and I invite you to create and implement more of your own, using your imagination, expertise, and your own lived experiences as part of the learning journey. My hope in preparing this selection of activities and sharing them is to inspire thought and action and to model methods to cultivate the conversation about race and identity, overall. We can then further apply our foundational teachings to the specific case of supporting the identity development of multiracial and multiethnic children.

What do we focus on? How do we integrate it into our existing curriculum plan? How do we ensure activities are age-appropriate?

An excellent model for offering age-appropriate standards for introducing concepts related to the understanding of self and other, racial difference, justice, and societal action is the "Social Justice Standards" developed by Teaching Tolerance.[2] These standards are developed around four key themes of Identity, Diversity, Justice and Action (IDJA). These standards can be used by teachers to support curriculum development, as well as by administrators and other leaders to guide school environments to be "just, equitable, and safe." Because the standards are developed for K–12 educational levels, activities designed around these standards are fully age-appropriate and can follow a child's development from year to year. These IDJA domains, based on Louise Derman-Sparks's four goals for anti-bias education in early childhood,[3] allow "educators to engage a range of anti-bias, multicultural and **social justice** issues"[4] as well as support collective action and consciousness-raising regarding key issues for underrepresented groups.

Let's explore these standards in the context of how to support and approach teaching about racial identity generally, as well as multiracial identity development in children.

The following are learning outcomes based upon grade level, with K–12 outcomes shared based on the four anchors of Identity, Diversity, Justice and Action. As you read through these guidelines, consider: how can these help guide activities to support children's understanding about race overall, and also identity development for multiracial children specifically?

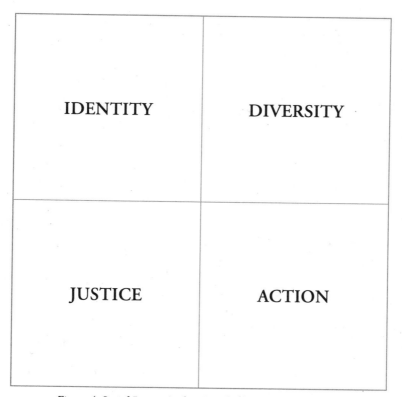

Figure 4. Social Justice Anchor Standards, Teaching Tolerance

Identity

1. Students will develop positive social identities based on their membership in multiple groups in society.

2. Students will develop language and historical and cultural knowledge that affirm and accurately describe their membership in multiple identity groups.

3. Students will recognize that people's mutable identities interact and create unique and complex individuals.

4. Students will express pride, confidence and healthy self-esteem without denying the value and dignity of other people.

5. Students will recognize traits of the dominant culture, their home culture and other cultures and understand how they negotiate their own identity in multiple spaces.

Diversity

6. Students will express comfort with people who are both similar to and different from them and engage respectfully with all people.

7. Students will develop language and knowledge to accurately and respectfully describe how people (including themselves) are both similar to and different from each other and others in their identity groups.

8. Students will respectfully express curiosity about the history and lived experiences of others and will exchange ideas and beliefs in an open-minded way.

9. Students will respond to diversity by building empathy, respect, understanding and connection.

10. Students will examine diversity in social, cultural, political and historical contexts rather than in ways that are superficial or oversimplified.

Justice

11. Students will recognize stereotypes and relate to people as individuals rather than representatives of groups.

12. Students will recognize unfairness on the individual level (e.g., biased speech) and injustice at the institutional or systemic level (e.g., discrimination).

13. Students will analyze the harmful impact of bias and injustice on the world, historically and today.

14. Students will recognize that power and privilege influence relationships on interpersonal, intergroup and institutional levels and consider how they have been affected by those dynamics.

15. Students will identify figures, groups, events and a variety of strategies and philosophies relevant to the history of social justice around the world.

Action

16. Students will express empathy when people are excluded or mistreated because of their identities and concern when they themselves experience bias.

17. Students will recognize their own responsibility to stand up to exclusion, prejudice and injustice.

18. Students will speak up with courage and respect when they or someone else has been hurt or wronged by bias.

19. Students will make principled decisions about when and how to take a stand against bias and injustice in their everyday lives and will do so despite negative or peer pressure.

20. Students will plan and carry out collective action against bias and injustice in the world and will evaluate what strategies are most effective.

These standards are reprinted with permission of Teaching Tolerance, a project of the Southern Poverty Law Center. You can find out more about this and other resources at www.tolerance.org.

What's wonderful about these standards is that the way they are developed and positioned leaves much room for a person who is multiracial to explore membership in multiple groups, and also learn about oneself and others, with the freedom to shift, change, and react in different ways. An important part of any educational effort is to note the fluidity of identity that can occur with multiracial individuals, and also be present to identity development as a process of exploration, reaction, learning, and increasing understanding. It is in no way fixed, static, immovable, or fully determined by one variable; it is a combination of factors that contribute to a whole sense of self. Additionally, the connection to social justice and community action initiatives allows for expression against injustice, which therefore empowers individuals who may feel excluded or marginalized because of their difference. Overall, these age-appropriate standards are tremendously effective guides for teachers looking to cultivate learning experiences in the classroom for all children—with the benefit of these being in alignment with supportive multiracial identity experiences. Parents and caregivers can also be mindful of these standards and align experiences at home or out in the community, and also dialogue with their children, to match these anchor themes and developmental stages of exploration of these topics that are listed comprehensively in Appendix B.

Sample Teaching Activities

Here, I have included a few sample teaching activities that you can use to practice introducing racial and multiracial identity development with children in your care. We have to begin at the beginning. No understanding about multiracial identity can be achieved without an exploration of race and racial differences at the same time. Once the foundation of trust and comfort with the general topic of race has been established, you can move into deeper dialogue and push the conversation further to include even more of the social justice standards and learning objectives mentioned previously.

Some notes:

These activities are written for classroom teachers, but can be adapted to be done in the home by parents and caregivers.

The intended audience includes both multiracial and monoracial children, beginning with general topics of discussion about race, then integrating the opportunity to focus on the mixed-race experience specifically.

"Extension" activities are shared to further learning and dialogue, depending upon the readiness of both the adult and the child.

The "Education Standards Addressed" coding links to the list of Social Justice Standards by Teaching Tolerance that are mentioned in this chapter, and that are listed in detail by grade level in Appendix B.

Chapter 8 describes the action and advocacy needed when designing curriculum for and teaching multiracial children.

More lesson plan activities are shared in Appendix C of this book.

Grade Level: *K–5*

Title: *"Welcoming All"*

Subjects: *Art, Language Arts*

Education Standards Addressed: ID.K-2.1 TO ID.K-2.10, JU.K-2.11, AC.K-2.17 TO AC.K-2.20, ID.3-5.1, ID.3-5.4, ID.3-5.6, ID.3-5.8, DI.3-5.9, AC.3-5.17, AC.3-5.19, AC.3-5.20

Learning Objectives
Cultivating an environment of inclusion, trust, and belonging at the beginning of the school year.

Resource
All Are Welcome by Alexandra Penfold and Suzanne Kaufman (2018)

Activities

1. Read the book with the class. Ask the children what differences they notice and appreciate.

2. Invite discussion about children's own differences, highlighting multiracial identity or intersectionality as it comes up.

3. Create a brainstormed list with the group of what will help each child feel included in the class. This can be the basis for "community norms" for the class.

4. Discuss what impact, consequences, and outcomes can occur if any of these agreements, norms, or needs are not kept up by the class. Envision what the experience of the group will look like if these community norms are upheld. Invite the children to draw a symbol of what it feels like to feel happy or included (sun, flowers, pets, rainbow, etc.).

5. Print out photos of each child, post the illustrations they drew, and create a word cloud of the list of things brainstormed that support the inclusion of each child. Put these up on a bulletin board with a title such as "We welcome you!"

Extension: Advocacy and Activism

1. Read *Say Something!* by Peter H. Reynolds (2019).

2. Discuss how speaking up can help express one's own feelings and needs, and also how it can help make the world better for others.

3. Connect back to community agreements and the vision for the group.

4. At a later date, tie in this idea of "saying something" to a cause or action that the class or school is supporting (e.g., clean water, families in need, etc.).

Grade Level: *K–3*

Title: *"We're All Different!"*

Subjects: *Art, Language Arts, Social Studies*

Education Standards Addressed: ID.K-2.1, ID.K-2.3, ID.K-2.4, ID.K-2.6, ID.K-2.7, ID.3-5.1, ID.3-5.4, ID.3-5.6

Learning Objectives

Encouraging children to notice and explore differences and fostering the understanding that differences are normal and are a strength.

Cultivating self-identity and confidence in children about their own distinct traits and sense of self.

Resources

The Colors of Us by Karen Katz (1999)

Shades of People by Shelley Rotner and Sheila M. Kelly (2009)

The Colors of the Rainbow by Jennifer Moore-Mallinos (2005)

We're Different, We're the Same by Bobbi Jane Kates (1992)

Supplies

Multicultural crayons or colored pencils

Multicultural construction paper

Activities

1. Read one or more of the above books. Talk about the differences mentioned in the books, utilizing guiding questions that address what noticeable traits the child has that are the same as or different from others around them.

2. Emphasize that noticing differences is not bad, but treating people differently and worse because of the differences is a problem.

3. Explain that food is used as a comparison in *The Colors of Us* to explain the different shades of skin tones. Ask, "What is your skin tone like?" Explain that calling people names based on food or other objects is not okay, but as a comparison for expressing ideas is great. Encourage positive interactions as you discuss differing skin tones. *Option:* As a class, create a board with glued-on items (e.g., sand, tree bark) for children to compare their skin tone to.

4. The children create a picture of themselves using multicultural crayons or colored pencils, or by cutting out multicultural construction paper. The children can utilize textured materials such as string or fabrics to add more texture to their piece.

5. *Optional closing:* Read Shel Silverstein's poem "Colors" from the book *Where the Sidewalk Ends* (2002). Talk about the meaning of the last line: "And all the colors I am inside / Have not been invented yet" as inspiration for children to dream about who they want to be, beyond any physical appearance or limits.

Extension: Multiracial Identity

1. Read the book *Honeysmoke: A Story of Finding Your Color* by Monique Fields (2019).

2. Explain how this family is made up of different cultures and races, and introduce that a child from a family of different races is called multiracial. (Beforehand, practice how you will share the definition of race and culture that is age-appropriate and so that you are comfortable with sharing with the children.)

3. Invite brainstorming by the children about their own "color word" combination of words or a phrase that can describe themselves, sharing examples from the book such as sun quartz, arctic pearl, or your own (such as brick cloud, summer siren, onyx dream, etc.).

4. Have the children write their color words as a part of or next to their self-portraits.

Grade Level: *6–8, 9–12*

Title: *"Identity and Representation"*

Subjects: *Language Arts, Social Studies, Art*

Education Standards Addressed: ID.6-8.1 through ID.6-8.9, JU.6-8.11, JU.6-8.14, JU.6-8.17, DI.9-12.1 through DI.9-12.10, JU.9-12.11, JU.9-12.12, JU.9-12.14, AC.9-12.16 through AC.9-12.20

Learning Objectives

Understanding the multiple layers of one's own identity, and multiracial identity, and how it can change over time.

Resources

Mixed: Portraits of Multiracial Kids by Kip Fulbeck (2010)

Part Asian, 100% Hapa by Kip Fulbeck (2006)

Hāfu2Hāfu by Tetsuro Miyazaki (2019)

Mixed Blood by CYJO (2014)

hapa.me: 15 years of the hapa project by Kip Fulbeck (2018)

Blended Nation: Portraits and Interviews of Mixed-Race America by Mike Tauber and Pamela Singh (2009)

Of Many Colors: Portraits of Multiracial Families by Gigi Kaeser (1994)

Activities

1. In small groups, students review one or more of the above books and take turns sharing a page from the book and reading out loud or showing the self-identifying descriptions by each

person or family photographed. (*Mixed: Portraits of Multiracial Kids* and *Part Asian, 100% Hapa* by Kip Fulbeck are recommended for younger age groups; all books are recommended for older age groups.) Explain the term "Hapa," its original meaning from Hawaiian culture and language, and how that meaning has been used by different groups over time.

2. While reflecting on what they have just seen and read, students individually draw a picture, using colored pencils or crayons, of a story or experience related to identity in their own life, which can be inspired by the books they just read or by something completely different.

3. Using a story circle format, students then take turns sharing the story or experience related to their identity, with no commentary by other members of the group, except for a respectful "thank you" after each person has shared.

4. Once each person has shared, students can spontaneously share their reactions to other people's stories as well as the books that they have read and the portraits they have viewed.

5. In a larger group or as a class, invite students to share what they felt themselves, or noticed from both their individual experiences or their group. Ensure that students speak about their own experiences, and not on behalf of others, unless they have permission.

6. The teacher can share photos from the *hapa.me* book to show how identity has stayed the same or changed over time. Ask students, "How is identity challenged and contested, just like the term Hapa itself?" Debrief further.

Extension: Portraits of Me

Using a Polaroid or other instant camera, take student portraits and ask them to write a self-description, similar to those of the participants in Kip Fulbeck's books, to go along with the photo. Post the portraits on a bulletin board or make a binder of the portraits as a classroom exhibit that can be brought home by each student for a few days each year.

Extension: Questions and Thoughts

Have students choose one question from the *Hāfu2Hāfu* book and write a one-page answer accompanied by a Polaroid photo of themselves. Invite them to share an additional question to ask their peers and classmates, as a part of their writing project.

SELF-REFLECTION

When you see these sample lesson plans, how do you react? Are these activities that you think you can share with children in your classroom or at home? What are some aspects of the lesson that would work with your teaching style and student group, and what do you think would be a challenge? Reflecting back on your own readiness, as well as issues that are present when we examine and live out racial categorizations, what difficulty do you see in inviting this conversation? Also, are there larger systemic dynamics at play at school or in the home that would potentially be a barrier to an open conversation about race? How can this be overcome?

Reflect on your responses and think through what is needed to make a learning program about racial identity and multiracial identity successful for the children in your care, as well as for yourself as the educator and facilitator.

Write down an action plan including follow-up items to continue curriculum design and to access support and resources around this topic.

7

From College to Career

THIS CHAPTER LOOKS at the experiences that may occur post–high school for your children—in the form of higher-education enrollment and also the beginning of one's professional career. It is important to note that there is not an assumption that one will go to college *and then* begin a career. These are both major milestones that can be independent of one another, yet also mark major areas of impact on your child's continued racial identity development. The assertion of independence, and the exposure to many different ideas, people, lifestyles, and experiences, will launch your child further down the path of exploration of and increased decision making about their own identity preference and their expression of their own identity development. The campus and the workplace are two locations where much formation of identity occurs, beyond the formal learning experiences of K–12 schooling.

College/University

Preparing to go to college is no easy feat, and the choice of higher-education institution that your college-ready child is going to attend is no light decision. In order to continue to support your child's multiracial identity through these impactful, formative years, it may be prudent for you and your family to consider a variety of factors, from academic to co-curricular activities, that emphasize this important aspect of your child's development.

Things to consider for your child's choice of institution and involvement in activities, from the perspective of supporting multiracial identity, include data on the multiracial student population; academics; co-curricular activities, student life, and multicultural student services; multiracial representation in student affairs; special programs and recognition; conferences; and the general student experience.

Data on the Multiracial Student Population

Is this recorded and reported for the institution? What are the percentages of multiracial students within the population? How do these numbers translate into actual services or programs for multiracial individuals? It is useful to consider the makeup of the student body representing the monoracial communities that your child may identify with, and also representing the multiracial population. Ask your child how these demographics may affect them while they are attending this institution, and how they can prepare, with knowledge of the school population context. This exercise can help mentally prepare your child for the experiences that could come with attending a predominantly White institution (PWI), a historically Black college or university (HBCU), or an institution with either a lack of or an overrepresentation of a certain ethnic group. If this isn't discussed, your child may face this aspect of attending college as yet another thing to transition to, compounded by the fact that it may be a shock or surprise for them to see how it can be similar to or different from the neighborhood or community in which they themselves have grown up. Also, for universities and colleges that don't collect this data, this may be an indication of how programs and support services related to race are handled by the institution, in that there may be a deficit. With this data absent, we have unfortunately seen the onus put on students[1] to organize around this, rather than staff and administration or senior educational leadership taking the lead—for a variety of political, economic, or administrative reasons. It can be a barrier to a student's focus on their studies when their school environment is lacking in belonging for people like them.

Academics

Is there the opportunity for a student to take academic courses that explore race and identity overall, or for their specific cultural group? Some known scholars who offer incredible coursework on multiracial identity or integrate it into their curricular approach and research include Dr. Paul Spickard and Dr. Reginald Daniel (University of California, Santa Barbara), Dr. Rudy P. Guevarra Jr. and Dr. Kelly Faye Jackson (Arizona State University), Dr. Lily Anne Y. Welty Tamai (University of California, Los Angeles), Janet C. Mendoza Stickmon (Napa Valley College), Dr. Myra Washington (University of New Mexico), Dr. Curtiss Takada Rooks (Loyola Marymount University), Dr. Velina Hasu Houston (University of Southern California), Dr. Teresa Williams-León (California State University, Northridge), Dr. Sarah Gaither (Duke University), Dr. Diana Sanchez (Rutgers University), Dr. Lauren D. Davenport (Stanford University), Dr. Nitasha Tamar Sharma (Northwestern University), Dr. Stephen Murphy-Shigematsu (Stanford University), Dr. Marc P. Johnston-Guerrero (The Ohio State University), Camilla Fojas (University of Virginia), Laura Kina (DePaul University), Dr. Eric Hamako (Shoreline Community College), Dr. Francis Wardle (Red Rocks Community College), Dr. Kristin Pauker (University of Hawai'i at Mānoa), Dr. Naliyah Kaya (Montgomery College), Dr. Mitzi Carter (Florida International University), Dr. Ralina L. Joseph (University of Washington–Seattle), Dr. Greg

Carter (University of Wisconsin–Milwaukee), Dr. Minelle Mahtani (University of British Columbia), and Dr. Allison Briscoe-Smith (The Wright Institute), among many others. A special mention goes to faculty members Wei Ming Dariotis and Nicole Leopardo of San Francisco State University, the co-creators of the first and only Critical Mixed Race Studies minor! The process of creating this minor had input from the College of Ethnic Studies (Africana Studies, Latina/Latino Studies, Asian American Studies, American Indian Studies, and Race and Resistance Studies), which allows students to receive a "critical and comparative understanding of the various intersecting histories of different groups." An important part of the Critical Mixed Race Studies minor is the new course "Transracial Adoptee Experience," created by Kira Donnell with support from Sophie McHenry Navarro. This is by no means an exhaustive list, and individuals may change institutions or focus areas. Although I am unable to know and list everyone who is in the field doing tremendous work around multiracial identity, my hope is that this sample showcases the impactful contributions by scholars, researchers, and faculty in the field so we may seek them and others out to support and learn from their expertise.

Co-curricular Activities, Student Life, and Multicultural Student Services

Does the college offer support to students through caucus or student service associations dedicated to specific ethnic groups, and multiracial students in particular? How do demographics-based sororities and fraternities receive individuals of mixed race heritage? What general campus activities reflect inclusion and support belonging of multiracial students?

Many higher-education institutions have demographic-based student groups and centers on campuses (e.g., the Latinx Coalition, the Native American Student Association, the AAPI Exchange, Black Students' Union, etc.), or even a Multicultural Student

Services Center to address the needs of BIPOC students. In any of those spaces, is there an active effort to mention that multiracial people are welcome, in an overt and visible way? It is important to have this "declaration of multiracial inclusion" frequently, as new members join, and to regularly reiterate that the space is welcoming for individuals who identify with more than one racial background. Note: saying that a space is "welcome to all" is not enough. It is important to make sure this is specifically called out in order to name the issue, bring more attention to it, and build up to addressing it directly within programming and events.

Here is a sample model of a "declaration of multiracial inclusion":

Hello all! My name is Cynthia. My pronouns are she/her/hers. Welcome to the first meeting of the AAPI Student Exchange. This group was formed to support the needs of Asian Americans and Pacific Islanders on campus. This includes individuals of multiracial or multiethnic heritage, and also transracial adoptees. We look forward to our year of programs and events with you!

It may be worthwhile to explore if there is a multiracial student association that exists on campus, and how active they currently are—given that leadership is constantly in flux and the activity level can depend upon the student governance that is in place at the time. A search of the institution's website or a general social media search can reveal some information about which groups exist on campus. Some examples of such organizations are MiXed at Cornell, Multiracial Biracial Student Association (MBSA) at the University of Maryland–College Park, Multiracial Student Union (MSU) at the University of Minnesota, Mixed Student Union at UCLA, Mixed Student Union at the

University of Illinois at Urbana-Champaign, McGill University Multiracially Open Students Association (MUMOSA), and the recently founded Coalition of Multiracial and Biracial Students (COMBS) at the University of Puget Sound. Another possible resource to explore further is the National Association of Mixed Student Organizations (NAMSO), which unites mixed heritage student organizations across the United States. Through connecting with these student organizations and networks, one can link up with the local initiatives that are found at an institution or in a geographic region. This can serve as an outlet for a multiracial college student to continue exploring their identity and align with others who are navigating similar experiences.

What if no group like this exists on campus, or has gone inactive? Would your child be willing and motivated to lead one? Andy Riemer shared with me[2] how he and Anri Wheeler reestablished a multiracial group at Harvard in 2017, after they met during the Students of Color Orientation for the Harvard Graduate School of Education. He described how they "reflected on their own identity as well as the desire for a place to refill their cup through shared identity and discussions of the diversity within multi-racial identities." As a result, they reinvigorated, renamed, and co-led MIXED (Multiracial Individuals eXchanging and Encouraging Dialogue) at Harvard[3] that culminated in a year-end event focused on interracial relationships that continued as an **affinity group.**

Groups such as these can create a tremendous sense of belonging and support, in the midst of a potentially difficult transition to the college way of life.

Multiracial Representation in Student Affairs

Is there a presence of individuals within student affairs and school administrative leadership who are forthright in supporting multiracial identities within mainstream environments? Some extremely supportive advocates of multiracial identity within higher education include Charlene Martinez (Oregon State University), Jennifer Wells (Scripps College), and Sabrina T. Kwist (Los Medanos College), among others. Creating connections with supportive leaders and advocates such as these would be beneficial for mentorship and involvement in programs and activities that will enhance the student experience.

Beyond connecting with individual leaders, what groups and networks exist that can be an outlet for individuals who identify with more than one race, as a multiracial individual in college administration?

One powerful network to leverage related to student affairs is the Multiracial Network (MRN), which is one of five networks within the Coalition for Multicultural Affairs (CMA) of the American College Personnel Association (ACPA). The mission of MRN is to provide resources and information about working with multiracial college students as well as support for multiracial student affairs professionals within ACPA.

Another organized group to explore is the NASPA Multi-Racial Knowledge Community (MRKC), which is a part of the National Association of Student Personnel Administrators. The mission of MRKC is to "advocate on behalf of multiracial and mixed-heritage (hereafter collectively referred to as multiracial), and transracial adoptee individuals, support those who work with/educate multiracial and adopted students, and gain a visible presence within NASPA."[4]

As youth move into student affairs or campus leadership roles, they will also need support in their continued personal identity development, as well as navigating their careers as multiracial individuals. Who can be their role models, or allies and partners, in continuing to create spaces for conversation about multiracial identity? These networks can be extremely valuable in locating others who are on the same journey and who can be collaborators with and mentors to your multiracial child.

Special Programs and Recognition

A very unique part of the college experience is being able to take part in programs that build community and bring people together. For multiracial students, it is such a valuable opportunity to connect with others who share the experience of having multiple heritages. One notable program that invites multiracial students to explore their identity while building community is Multiracial Aikido[5] held at Oregon State University. The purpose of this retreat is to "increase understanding of one's multiracial identities; explore the role of physical appearance and family; and build community with other students and staff." This unique program, inspired by Oregon State University's "Racial Aikido," "harnesses the principles of aikido to recognize, respond, and replenish."[6] The phenomenal resources and facilitation of this program were guided by the leadership of individuals such as Charlene Martinez and her colleagues Jonathan Stoll, Melinda Shell, Kim McAloney, and Stephanie Shippen, among others. For many students, as Charlene describes, "it is the first time they are grappling with their identities and mixedness" and is "an experiential learning exchange that is ... a place to share stories. It is a place to connect with self."[7]

A notable award program at the University of Maryland–College Park is the Mildred & Richard Loving Award.[8] This is given to a University of Maryland undergraduate student who has "demonstrated a significant and ongoing commitment to multiracial and cross-cultural causes and communities" and is named in honor of the couple at the heart of the landmark 1967 Supreme Court decision that invalidated anti-miscegenation laws in the United States.

At the time of writing, the University of California, Los Angeles hosts the only Mixed Alumni Association, founded in 2015 by Jenifer Logia with the mission "to build, support, and strengthen a community around mixed heritage identity."[9] The UCLA Mixed Alumni Association connects UCLA alumni and their families with future alumni and the overall UCLA community to "share their experiences, explore, and celebrate mixed heritage identity." This association organizes a number of gatherings for social connections, dialogue, and fundraisers for scholarships for mixed students and is a way for alumni who are multiracial to stay connected with one another.

Programs and recognitions such as these acknowledge the presence and contributions of multiracial individuals at the college level, and create a legacy that connects the past to the present, forging a path for the future. These are just a few examples, and it is worth exploring if the higher-education institution of choice has its own program supporting multiracial students. Although programs centering on multiracial identity are rare, they are incredibly important in honoring the existence and impact of multiracial students, staff, and faculty, contributing to an overall culture of belonging and inclusion for multiracial and multiethnic individuals.

Conferences

Conferences are a fantastic outlet for individuals to deepen knowledge and dialogue regarding multiracial identity. The Critical Mixed Race Studies (CMRS) conference,[10] founded in 2010 by Camilla Fojas, Laura Kina, and Wei Ming Dariotis, is hosted by higher-education institutions roughly every two years and led by a group of committed individuals who serve on the board and represent academia, the arts, activists, community members, and a variety of general members interested in this mission. CMRS is membership based. The MidWest Mixed[11] community was founded in 2014 by Alissa Paris and Owen Duckworth as a series of dialogue spaces for mixed race people in the Midwest. With a growing community and interest, the first MidWest Mixed Conference was held in 2017, a Kaleidoscope summer social event was held in 2018, and another conference was held in 2019. These events have a variety of themes and host conversations that include exploring a personal sense of

self, mental health, storytelling and narrative, resistance, the politics of identity, and more.

Past and ongoing events that have been instrumental in forming foundational relationships and dialogue within the multiracial
community include the Mixed Roots Film and Literary Festival
founded by Fanshen Cox and Heidi Durrow; the Mixed Remixed
Festival founded by Heidi Durrow, which focuses on the film and
literary works by and about the mixed race community; the Loving
Day Conference, which commemorated the fiftieth anniversary of
the landmark decision of *Loving v. Virginia;* and the Hapa Japan
Conference, which is a part of the Hapa Japan Project,[12] focusing
on the study of mixed race and mixed roots Japanese people glob-
ally. In Canada, the Hapa-palooza Festival[13] gathers artists, writers,
community members, and the general public to celebrate mixed
identity. The festival was founded by Anna Ling Kaye, Jeff Chiba
Stearns, and Zarah Martz, and its events are organized by the
Hybrid Ancestry Public Arts Society (HAPAS).

There are many other regional events that are held that honor
and celebrate the mixed race community and also dive deeper into an
exploration about multiracial identity. Another avenue to explore is
general interest conferences or professional association gatherings that
have caucuses or affinity groups based on demographics, including the
multiracial community. A partial listing of these can be found in chapter 9. What academic or professional interests does your child have?

General Student Experience

What other aspects of the student experience are important to
your child? Be sure to check out the diversity programs and support services offered in areas such as athletics, music, study abroad,
and others. It is important to understand how these programs are
designed and framed around demographics and the identities that
they serve, as this will undoubtedly impact the experiences your
child has within the institution of higher learning.

QUESTIONS FOR MULTIRACIAL STUDENTS TO ASK ABOUT COLLEGES AND UNIVERSITIES

- **Data:** What demographic data is available on the multiracial population?

- **Academics:** What coursework is available to further exploration of multiracial identity?

- **Co-curricular Activities:** What programs, activities, and organized groups are available for multiracial students? For demographic-based groups and centers, is there a "declaration of multiracial inclusion" mentioned in the group's charter or in person at events?

- **Student Affairs:** What administrative leaders are advocates for multiracial understanding and belonging? What networks can be tapped into for further support, mentorship, and collaboration?

- **Special Programs:** Are there special programs that recognize or enhance multiracial student involvement?

- **Conferences:** Is the higher-education institution a host or supporter of conferences focusing on the mixed race experience? When researching the location of the college, are there regional multiracial events to participate in?

- **General Student Experience:** What other aspects of the college/university experience and overall educational environment would impact a multiracial student's learning experience?

Career

When our multiracial children move into the job market, what resources are available for them to continue exploration and affirmation of their multiracial identity? It is erroneous to think that the needs and issues related to identity development finish as soon as children cross the threshold into independent careers and early adulthood.

As a diversity, equity, and inclusion consultant, I have been exposed to a wide variety of efforts that companies make to promote inclusion within a given organization. There could be an organization-wide strategy that is a push toward acknowledging diversity and cultivating inclusion within the workplace, or there could be the beginnings of some events or programs that are specifically targeted toward certain demographics, to cater to the needs of employees through support and community-building. From my experience working with Fortune 500 companies, startups, higher-education institutions, nonprofit organizations, and schools, I can wholeheartedly say that there is not a single cookie-cutter approach to how diversity, equity, and inclusion are addressed within the workplace. Also, there is a tremendous degree of difference in terms of how deep organizations are ready and willing to go to address inclusion and equity directly. Given that, it is important to do some investigation into what principles of diversity, equity, and inclusion are openly shared at a company, and how those commitments are expressed and upheld through actions and an actual path forward. There are a vast number of opportunities for individuals to get plugged into a career path that not only fulfills their aspirations within a certain industry, but also honors and acknowledges their identities in the workplace environment.

One of the ultimate goals of initiatives related to inclusion and belonging is to help create a space where employees can feel that they can bring their best, most authentic, and whole selves to work. It is a challenge when the dominant majority culture in many companies in North America is based on Western, capitalistic, individualistic, and patriarchal conceptions of leadership and success that favor those privileged identities. That being said, there is a movement toward understanding how a true honoring and leveraging of diversity comes with creating a working environment where all members of the workplace feel appreciated and whose identities are valued and not ignored. There are a number of forces that contribute to this cause, and that are of specific interest to multiracial individuals, especially as there still continues to be the need to navigate spaces where the frame of reference largely comes from an acceptance of monoracial identities as the default in the definition of diversity—though we know that is not representative of the entire population. The growing appreciation for intersectionality within identities is a significant step in the direction of acknowledging multiplicity and complexity that can exist in one person—as long as it hearkens to the original intended definition coined by Kimberlé Crenshaw as demonstrating the compounding of marginalization, rather than a mere superficial "glossing over" of the experience as positive and that "everyone is multifaceted." That all being said, we must also be wary of the potential discrimination that can occur as a result of the prevalence of White supremacy, anti-Blackness, bias, marginalization, and systemic oppression that regularly occurs in society and that is historically and unconsciously baked into organizations. As conscious as we are of these forces at play, workplaces do not escape these issues. In order to prepare adequately for a career in the workforce as a multiracial individual, the foundational work in identity exploration is critical to create self-confidence, strength, and a stable foundation, along with an awareness of what opportunities and roadblocks could potentially be present as one begins their career.

Let's explore some concrete aspects of the world of work that multiracial individuals may directly encounter as they move into a career.

Employee Resource Groups

A fantastic resource and gathering place for individuals at organizations is **employee resource groups,** also known as ERGs. ERGs are usually founded by the organization to support the collective, or may be formed by the coming together of individuals of the same demographic background—e.g., individuals who identify as African American, Asian, Latinx, **LGBTQ+,** parents, veterans, differently abled, and so on. ERGs serve as a source for community-building within an organization, provide a place for learning and career advancement, and can also act as an outreach and advocacy arm in partnership with social causes and charitable organizations. An expansion of affinity groups, ERGs are often leveraged as focus groups and resources for input on marketplace positioning, or as a source for tapping talent in the career pipeline. These groups are actively funded by most organizations who wish to support inclusion and engagement of employees at work. Business resource groups, known as BRGs, are a development of ERGs to more directly align with business objectives of the organization while still holding the focus and engagement of the demographic group.

Although the benefits of ERGs are evident to both the employee who identifies with a group, and the company that supports them—what about multiracial individuals? Where do *they* belong? How do they fit into these neatly prescribed categories designed to be inclusive, but that can actually be oppressive, because it is yet *another* **forced choice?** Most organizations have an open participation policy, whereby anyone can attend any ERG they wish to, if a person feels comfortable doing so and is in support of the group's mission. I have witnessed many allies and advocates who don't identify directly as a part of the ERG's mandated demographic but have served in leadership positions, or as active volunteers, in support of the group. The difference with multiracial individuals is there can be a questioning about belonging within a group—by both the individual and the group—even though it is not said outwardly.

On the part of the multiracial individual, there can be an enhanced state of self-consciousness about belonging within a group, feeling "enough" to fit into the group—and also personal conflict if one feels there is judgment from others in the group.

Although ERGs are designed to be inclusive and have missions stating that is the case, because there is a formidable lack of multiracial ERGs within organizations as well as a lack of multiracial leaders who feel comfortable actively expressing their identity on a public platform due to society's comfort with and predisposition toward monoracial identification, a multiracial individual may still feel they need to posture or prove their identity within the group. Of course, that is not the case with every individual or every group. It is a positive outcome to have the opportunity to connect with others of the same community affiliation. However, this speaks to the larger question of how multiracial individuals are systematically underserved and overlooked. I have heard of extremely rare occasions of multiracial ERGs existing within companies. Most of the time, they can be lumped into overall "multicultural" or "D&I" ERGs or committees that serve as a catch-all for individuals who don't fit into other demographic groups. The case may be made that there isn't a critical mass—but given the size of some of the companies I have worked with, I can't believe that there isn't the population for these groups to exist. I believe the reasons behind this are a combination of the propensity toward monoracial identification and accepted definitions of identities with single-race categories by the general public and, by extension, organizations; and "covering" by multiracial individuals who wish to proclaim monoracial identities for a host of reasons, including but not limited to needing to fit in, not fully having an actualized multiracial sense of self, shame, lack of understanding, or ease. In summary, most organizations don't provide the structure for multiracial identity to be openly understood and realized, and many multiracial individuals don't see multiracial identity as a possibility or favored choice, given these constraints. One action step is for the leaders of these ERGs to directly and outwardly declare that the space is welcome for everyone, including those of mixed ethnic heritage.

I recall being at a conference where there were ERG breakout sessions organized by ethnic affiliation. I chose not to go to the Asian one, but instead went to the combined multicultural/multiracial one. I was so pleased to see that offering on the conference agenda at all. Within this group were individuals who were expats, Arab Americans who didn't fit into other categories, and also individuals who were biracial and multiracial. It was a coming together of different aspects of diversity and multiple identities. Although I appreciated that space, I found that because it was a mash-up of so many different communities into one group, it really didn't serve any one group fully. Multiracial individuals definitely had specific experiences that were surfaced but not deeply processed due to the arrangement of this meeting, and due to the combination with those who were not multiracial. This was extremely frustrating and dissatisfying, especially being a participant who was looking forward to "being with my group" in a space intentionally carved out for that community-building. Again, one could point to the lack of critical mass to warrant a separate multiracial meeting—but there were other monoracial demographic groups that had fewer attendees, and still had their own separate space *and* an invitation to the public to participate. Do you see how the systemic structures limit our ability to fully live out a multiracial identity?

Dr. Sarah Gaither explains how "Research has shown that children and adults who feel like they are forced to choose one of their racial or ethnic identities over the other are more likely to have negative mental health consequences. Thus, allowing a multiracial child to freely explore their own racial and ethnic identities should lead to more positive outcomes without that added pressure of having to choose."[14]

For your multiracial child, they can therefore choose to belong to one or more ERGs at an organization, or—with enough collective momentum—can venture to start their own multiracial ERG. Let them know that the choice of affiliation is an option for them, in spite of any pressure or expectation they may feel to identify one way or another. Although certain ERGs may be suggested to them based on demographic information they choose to disclose upon hiring, they can opt-in to any group at any time. Reinforce the freedom of choice and participation, and also in forging a new path to creating spaces for themselves, in the absence of a dedicated space for multiracial individuals. ERGs are a growing space and something to pay attention to, as a multiracial individual determines their own involvement and direction with a company.

Entrepreneurship

A path many individuals are choosing now for a productive career is that of entrepreneurship. The freedom and flexibility that come with entrepreneurship meet the needs of exploring one's creative passions, and align with the tide of how work is moving quickly to the norm of a gig economy. Becoming a business owner could be an optimal choice for your child. One opportunity available to entrepreneurs is that of minority business certification, which gives minority-certified individuals access to contract opportunities from companies and government entities, to do business through a pathway designed to support underrepresented businesses. This avenue of accessing business opportunities is called supplier diversity. As a diverse supplier, you are able to bid for contract opportunities and have that minority certification as an additional aspect of your qualifications that can help position you for extra training, support, and access.

How does one get minority certification? There are national and industry-based certification agencies that offer certification to minority business owners who have at least 51% ownership of the business, along with other key criteria. But how do you prove that you are a minority? What if you are multiracial? At what point does a multiple heritage ancestry count, or is no longer valid? This is particularly troubling in the multiracial community where one's identity can be called into question.

The idea of proving one's racial identity in the business setting has been met with controversy, as individuals who are not from underrepresented communities may take advantage of the supplier diversity program by falsifying company structure and organizational leadership in order to receive program benefits. This is what prompted the need for certification in the first place. A very prominent example of such controversy[15] has arisen regarding the claiming of Native American ancestry by individuals who "have no federal recognition and are considered illegitimate by recognized tribes and Native American experts." This battle over alleged illegitimate claims has been linked to a figure of more than $300 million in government contracts when accounting for what went to potentially unsubstantiated claims of Native American ownership. These numbers are staggering. That being said, who can determine if these are false claims to Indigenous heritage or not? Who are the gatekeepers of identity? Consequently, what is troubling is how the fluidity of racial identity can put multiracial individuals at risk for even more increased scrutiny. It also begs the larger question: how does one prove membership in an underrepresented racial category? Do DNA ancestry tests now count toward that? How does this affect individuals who are already struggling with ownership of their identity? How do multiracial individuals, specifically of mixed White and BIPOC ancestry, navigate this, since these programs are geared toward individuals of color or Indigenous ancestry?

Although there may not be a clear answer, it is important to have awareness of the issues at hand so multiracial individuals can be prepared for the potential challenges that they may face. It is also important to pay attention to how laws and policies regarding these types of programs and benefits may shift over time. If you feel so inclined, you may be motivated to monitor and weigh in with your local elected official regarding any political bills related to minority business enterprise ownership that could affect future rulings in cases such as these. In any case, a multiracial individual should become aware of the nuances of entrepreneurship and needs-based or minority-based procurement and other business programs that need proof of the qualified minority status of the owners. How would this affect your multiracial child?

Lastly, being a founder, owner, or other leader in an entrepreneurial venture may mean that the individual is in the spotlight more than an individual contributor, manager, or other employee. So, the task of being a highly visible leader of the business itself is compounded with the public noticing who this person is, in leadership. There may be added curiosity and interest by the general public toward multiracial business leaders as to which group affiliation or identity that the leader chooses to align with more. With leadership comes the responsibility of being a role model. What choice will your child make about their own expression of identity, while in these type of roles? I recall seeing Ben Chestnut, CEO of MailChimp, speak at a business and leadership conference focused on recognition of and achievement by Asian American professionals. I was delighted and inspired to hear about his multiracial background, emphasizing in his story his Thai mother and White American father. His describing how his family made ends meet and also about his personal struggle of not fitting into either culture of his family is something that I treasured witnessing on such a broad stage, as it is not something often heard at these settings and it connected with me deeply. How will your multiracial child communicate about their identity while in the public spotlight as a business leader?

Co-working

Co-working spaces are proliferating, as the traditional methodology of sitting at an office desk is being replaced with remote working. Co-working spaces are becoming more than just a place to park your laptop, answer emails and bang out reports, or take phone calls. They are active spaces of engagement that focus on community-building among all patrons of their spaces. These spaces often have overarching missions that talk about serving and connecting members and contributing to the betterment of society. As a result of these larger goals about work, co-working spaces offer programs that approach issues dear to their members and the overall community. A co-working space can be a place for multiracial individuals to thrive and shape their work environment, and also for all individuals to come into contact with one another and learn about other walks of life that they hadn't previously been exposed to.

I have personally participated in events at co-working spaces that engage deeply with issues of DEI and that uplift voices around the intersectionality of identity, as well as multiraciality specifically. Events, panel discussions, and outreach campaigns focus on speaking to topics such as race, gender, sexuality, age, and other key topics that are defined as core issues. What's important about conversations and spaces like these is how the awareness-building and knowledge-sharing are all done with a dedication to social change. It models that all of us, even with our own individual identities and experiences, can come together toward understanding a core issue and can join the movement toward greater inclusion for all.

I encourage multiracial individuals who access co-working spaces to be on the lookout for programs that speak to these issues, or encourage the community managers at these locations to put on events that address these aspects of identity, and whether inclusion can affect how we work.

Employment Discrimination

A topic that is less spoken about or understood is how discrimination specific to multiracial individuals can surface and be experienced. The racialized world we live in can sometimes guide individuals to concede to a binary of Black and White, with anti-Blackness and pro-Whiteness as a norm that is unfortunately experienced in all aspects of life, including the workplace. How does a biracial or multiracial individual fit into these simplistic categorizations, especially when they often straddle these labels? Unfortunately, multiracial individuals still experience discrimination, with the added complexity of a multiple identity being misinterpreted by others or leading to suspicion about the individual's alliances. Legal scholar Tanya Katerí Hernández has documented denigrating examples of civil rights cases that multiracial individuals have endured.[16] The added salt in the wound is when those presiding over the case do not understand the multiplicity of identity, and how one can have a fluidity regarding a sense of self—and still be discriminated against.

One discriminatory workplace experience is of an individual who was hired by a store to be a sales associate, and witnessed racism against fellow African American employees by a manager. When the manager was informed that the sales associate was in fact biracial, the sales associate was spared being fired, and eventually was promoted. That associate still experienced hearing racist remarks against Black people over a prolonged period of time, refused to wrongfully terminate someone just due to their race, and was eventually terminated. The difficulty in this situation is how to prove that a person is indeed harmed and put into a disadvantaged position, even though they could be seen as more privileged than others. How can the justice system be helped to understand the complexity of the multiplicity of identity?

Another example of workplace discrimination against multiracial people is a police officer who phenotypically appears White, and took a DNA test that showed he has Black heritage. When this was shared with other members of his department, he was subject to racial epithets, constant disparaging remarks, and an eventual demotion. Although the case focused on anti-Black sentiment, an additional layer present and underexamined was how he, as a multiracial individual, moved from being a person presenting as White, to becoming othered and minoritized. Again, there is complexity and questioning around who belongs, what makes exclusion and marginalization happen, and how we examine and determine the depth of the impact of a discriminatory experience.

. Another case was a biracial Black and White woman who initially did not experience discrimination until her manager observed her Black family members and friends visiting her at the retail store, and then realized she had Black heritage. She was then subject to discriminatory comments and racially insulting remarks. The jury in the case did not grasp the scope of "passing as White" and then being discriminated against for being Black.

All of these cases of discrimination involve the added element of multiracial identity, and demonstrate how our legal system fails to recognize the holding of more than one identity at the same time. As Hernández explains, "Racial mixture is a presumed complication in anti-discrimination law." Experiences of the intersectionality of multiracial identities can compound, creating an even more problematic situation. The impact of the experience is further deepened by all parties in the legal system failing to acknowledge that the discrimination is actually based in what Hernández calls **anti-multiracial bias,** and instead defaults into classifying it into a case of anti-Blackness or discrimination against People of Color in general, which is terrible enough without the added burden of trying to explain how multiracial people are impacted by the burden of proving their identity, and that this was indeed discrimination in the first place.

What is important from these examples of discrimination is to understand that there is a uniqueness about multiracial identity that is not always covered in formalized conceptions of the law or human resources policies. As a result, a multiracial individual experiencing discrimination may find it difficult to express what is problematic about a situation, or to have the discriminatory aspects of the scenario fully understood. There may be an inner doubt and questioning about the validity of the experience that is hard to shake for a multiracial youth. As a society, we lean into the racial polarization that is generally taught, making it even more difficult to expand past these binary conceptions to carve out a space for the specific, complex experiences that multiracial people endure. As parents, caregivers, and educators, we can support children by listening and aiming to fully grasp the entirety of the multiracial experience of discrimination, and offering help to support the individual in framing the holistic nature of the incident, as it is uniquely experienced by a multiracial individual.

General Workplace Dynamics

Depending upon who their coworkers are, and the company's geographic location, your child may come into contact with coworkers and even managers and supervisors who are unfamiliar with multiracial identity or your child's particular ethnic background. As with any interaction and using the skills and approaches we have discussed previously, your child will arrive at a method that works best for them, in order to navigate workplace and office dynamics. The opportunity in being open to sharing understanding about multiracial identity is to create strong bonds with new colleagues and friends while working together. Of course, microaggressions and other aspects of a multiracial person's lived experience will also be present in the workplace setting. It is important to pay attention to specific interactions and instances, and monitor if any of these move into the realm of a human resources concern or discrimination, as was previously discussed.

CAREER CONSIDERATIONS
FOR THE MULTIRACIAL INDIVIDUAL

- **Employee Resource Groups:** At a company, what ERGs are available to an employee, and which are specifically geared to your child's racial identity? If there is no group representing the demographic your child is most aligned with, is there an opportunity to start a new group? Would your child be interested in leading/spearheading a current or potentially new ERG, if the opportunity was possible?

- **Entrepreneurship:** Is your child interested in starting their own enterprise? Would the industry and service/product they are offering be something that would benefit from minority supplier certification? If so, is your child prepared to position to the forefront the "minority" (BIPOC) aspect of their identity, due to the criteria and common understanding of ethnic identification that is required by the certification process? How does your child feel about that? How will your child choose to express their multiracial identity affiliations in public, since there is added attention and focus on them as an entrepreneur and business leader?

- **Co-working:** Is your child planning to work from home or a remote location, such as a co-working space? What programs, events, or activities does the local co-working space offer related to cultural and racial understanding? How can a person get involved, to open up and further dialogue about multiracial identity?

- **Employment Discrimination:** If your child experiences workplace discrimination, what avenues are there to report and escalate complaints? How open or aware would human resources and others be to understanding how an incident is related to anti-multiracial bias, rather than solely discriminating against a BIPOC person? How would your child react when faced with an instance of employment discrimination?

◈ **General Workplace Dynamics:** What is the demographic makeup of the company's geographic location, and how might this impact the organizational environment and understanding about multiracial identity? How is your child prepared to face microaggressions and other common experiences of multiracial individuals—but this time in the work setting? How will your child respond to curiosity about their multiracial identity? Will your child be open about it in larger platforms or opportunities to express it widely, in order to be a role model to others?

Action, Advocacy, and Community-Building

EFFECTS OF RACE are far-reaching, and this results in the need for advocacy regarding awareness and inclusion of multiracial identities. As a parent, caregiver, or educator who is informed about these issues, you may feel motivated to offer input on processes or speak for change to systems that are failing to acknowledge a multiracial person's full sense of self. Within this chapter, we will examine commonly experienced obstacles for multiracial children related to demographic forms and policies, multiracial identity and health, and curriculum and teaching. Additionally, we will look at the opportunities to deepen experiences and connections through continuing education and community-building. Each section of this chapter offers action items that can be implemented as potential steps to pursue equity, involvement, and positive impact for multiracial children.

Demographic Forms and Policies

When my first child was born, the hospital asked me to list the various ethnic identities that my child espoused. Fortunately, at the hospital where I was, I was able to choose more than one box regarding my son's race. I felt good about expressing the multitude of racial identities that my child was composed of.

With my second child, I don't recall filling out a form with a choice of race—never mind being able to choose multiple identities.

When needing to go to the hospital office years later, I happened to see on an intake form that my second child's racial identity was labeled as "White." Although my child has partial White European heritage, he is also Asian and phenotypically presents more as Asian. It was a compelling moment for me to find both the patience and the strength to advocate to acknowledge this part of my child's racial identity, especially while he was injured with a broken arm, the reason why we were at the hospital in the first place!

Fortunately, the school district we live in allows for the choice of more than one racial group when enrolling new students. However, a friend of mine who is in the next neighborhood but is part of a different city and school district has a forced choice where parents must choose a "primary race" on the form. My friend, a Japanese American woman married to a White American man, was puzzled by this forced choice, posted on Facebook a copy of the form, and asked her friends: what to do?

There is research[1] that shows that a forced-choice experience creates a dilemma for families. It is correlated with depressive symptoms in youth, and through this restriction of identity choice, also promotes beliefs in the greater society that a multiracial identity is devalued. In contrast, greater **identity autonomy** and greater public regard about one's identity predict greater psychological health.

Parents and educators can rally to give feedback to school districts and medical systems to allow for the option of more than one choice of racial identity on school and medical forms to allow for a more expansive expression of identity that is in alignment with the child's entire sense of being.

ACTION

Ensure that race questions on school applications, college applications, scholarship forms, health forms, and employment forms allow an individual to check more than one box. This is essential to send the message to multiracial individuals that this identity is visible and valued.

If you are a parent, caregiver, educator, or any other individual who comes across a form that does not allow for choosing more than one race:

- If your child is old enough, have a conversation with them about what this means, and nurture a discussion about choice and what a child would do or choose in that situation. Check in with how your child is feeling and what they are thinking, and offer support in the form of empathetic listening and dialogue. Reinforce how the child's identity is valued, even though they may not see themselves represented on the form.

- Give feedback to the institution that administered the form that this document is an inaccurate representation of racial identity, and it is communicating that a multiracial person's existence is devalued, dismissed, and stigmatized.

There was a major movement in the 1990s involving a variety of multiracial advocacy and nonprofit organizations regarding the right and ability to check more than one box on the US Census form.

The decision allowing for the ability to "check one or more" racial category beginning with the 2000 US Census still stands today. As a result of this landmark change, there is much data that can be extracted from census reports and American Community Surveys that can inform understanding about multiracial populations.

> ৯ In order for this collection of data to continue, the greater community must actively monitor and offer input into activities by the US government regarding the collection and reporting of data regarding census categories.

There also has been research,[2] and movements such as the Latinas and Latinos of Mixed Ancestry (LOMA) founded by Thomas Lopez, that create awareness of and advocacy regarding the limiting, binary category of checking "Hispanic or Latino" or "not Hispanic or Latino" on the US Census form. This binary category is limiting to an individual who is both at the same time and who doesn't accurately represent a multiethnic or multiracial person's identity. Also, there is much confusion in society about how to answer this question, because Latinx identity is listed as an ethnic category, rather than a racial one. Similarly, adding a Middle Eastern category has been considered. If this option were the case, then we would see a possible uptick in those who list more than one race, including Middle Eastern and White, thereby increasing the number of multiracial individuals counted in the US population. The impact of having a new category would be to further disaggregate larger racial categories such as "White" to offer finer detail as to which communities are in fact present, and therefore would allow us to look at the complexity of multiracial identity and how to better serve this vast community.

> ৯ It is important that community members and leaders take ownership of these potential policy changes and spread awareness about the possible impacts of such recategorization of racial groups.

ACTION

- ❧ Join movements around public policy to support multiracial individuals checking more than one box, or having their identities accurately depicted, on demographic forms. The reasoning for why existing policies remain may have to do with the perceived difficulty in collecting and processing data, or larger systemic practices that skew the results.

- ❧ Because you are a member of the community, sharing your voice regarding why those reasons are not valid and the problematic nature behind these practices will help move the needle in honoring the identities of multiracial individuals.

Multiracial Identity and Health

There are issues specific to multiracial identity with respect to overall health and medical care. Some of these issues are captured in the video *Race in Medicine: A Dangerous Prescription*,[3] which documents an event organized by the nonprofit Multiracial Americans of Southern California and the Mixed Student Union at UCLA, gathering expert panelists to discuss the impact of racial identity on health. Two of these panelists were Dr. Dorothy Roberts, an acclaimed scholar of race, gender, and the law, and a professor at the University of Pennsylvania; and Athena Mari Asklipiadis, founder and director of Mixed Marrow, an organization dedicated to finding bone marrow and blood cell donors for patients of multiethnic heritage.

In her TEDMED Talk, Dr. Dorothy Roberts speaks about the use of race in medical testing and diagnosis and how it can lead to "false biological predictions" in all areas of medical practice, including diagnoses, prescriptions, treatments, and how diseases are defined. In her talk, she recalls the problematic encounter she had before a medical test while filling out a form on race categories that didn't have the option to check more than one race, and explained how this could lead to skewed results. Dr. Roberts also speaks to how medical practices use race as a shortcut to determine prescriptive care and while conducting research, and how bias can be found in many points of the health care experience. Since race is a social construct, Dr. Roberts argues that the emphasis on race can blind doctors to other evidence-based measures (such as family history, muscle mass, enzyme levels, genetic traits, and family illnesses) that are often not analyzed in the moment of diagnosis. Additionally, she emphasizes how bias on the part of the health practitioner, as well as a lack of attention to systemic factors such as lack of health care access, physical, mental, and emotional impacts of racialized experiences, and other structural inequalities, can play a large part in health outcomes.

ACTION

- When your child is prescribed medicine or a treatment, find out more about this prescription and if the diagnosis was based on factors such as race. Clarify if there was an assumption based on the part of the health care provider about the child's racial background (i.e., mistakenly seen as a monoracial member of a particular racial group), based either on the perception of physical appearance, or on a form requested about your child's racial background.

- If the medicine prescribed has been proved in scientific trials to have certain outcomes based on race, ask or investigate how this could affect someone with a multiracial identity.

- Do not be afraid to ask questions or voice concerns at any point in the health care process. This is your child's health at stake.

Athena Mari Asklipiadis speaks about the challenges of patients of multiethnic heritage finding bone marrow and blood cell donors. Athena says, "Minority and mixed race patients face difficult odds in finding suitable donors when faced with a blood disease like leukemia, due to the donor pool lacking diversity."[4] She explains that "because tissue type and DNA markers matter in matching, most matches happen between people of the same or similar heritage." She describes how only about 4% of the US national donor registry is made up of mixed race donors, with most donors in the registry identifying as White.

Filmmaker Jeff Chiba Stearns created the film *Mixed Match,* which follows multiracial patients who are in need of a donor, as well as Mixed Marrow's efforts to support the process of locating a match for these patients. This touching documentary has been screened in film festivals in various countries and does a fantastic job of capturing the challenging journey that multiracial individuals are on when faced with a critical health condition dependent upon a bone marrow match.

ACTION

- Join a bone marrow registry near you, such as Be The Match, the US national bone marrow registry, or through ethnic-specific recruitment programs such as Pura Vida or Asians for Miracle Marrow Matches (A3M). It is as simple as filling out a form and taking a swab of the inside of your mouth. There are also bone marrow registry and donation programs in various countries around the world that you can locate and participate in.

- Support organizations such as Mixed Marrow through volunteering to host a donor registration drive, or by donating toward or fundraising for the cause. It is also helpful to follow social media channels and share stories of patients in need, to inspire others who have not yet registered with the donor registry.

𝕒 Watch the documentary film *Mixed Match* and talk with your child/children about this issue and how it affects the multiracial community specifically. Also, learn more about bone marrow donation to remove any fear or stigma about the process, as many procedures are noninvasive and participation in the program could save the life of someone else.

Curriculum and Teaching

How do the curriculum or teaching practices in schools capture the experiences of multiracial identity within the subjects that are being taught? There is an opportunity for the integration of ideas and activities that can highlight the normalcy of multiracial identity that can reinforce a positive sense of self for multiracial students and also increase the awareness of fellow classmates who are not multiracial themselves.

Dr. Geneva Gay, a professor of education at the University of Washington–Seattle and longtime educator, scholar, and author, has written extensively on "culturally responsive teaching." She explains this paradigm as teaching that "centers classroom instruction in multiethnic cultural frames of reference." In her book *Culturally Responsive Teaching: Theory, Research, and Practice,*[5] she shares "ideas for imagining and actualizing culturally responsive instruction."

Based on Dr. Gay's culturally responsive teaching ideas around "practice possibilities" (listed in bold), the following are my recommendations for reflective and purposeful educational strategies to engage multiracial learners. These strategies can be adopted by educators in the classroom, and also by parents and caregivers at home.

In addition, adults can advocate for these approaches to be incorporated into teaching plans within your child's classroom and school.

- **Engage in self-monitoring, self-regulation, and self-reflection.**
  Consider: "What do I know of my students' multiple cultures, how do I integrate resources from those cultures into my teaching plans, and what do my students already know about their own or other cultures?"

- **Don't depend on old assumptions.**
  Ask students to share about their lives and their cultures. Having students elaborate for themselves helps dispel any preexisting stereotypes or generalizations that you or their peers may have.

- **Get out of the classroom and go beyond the textbook.**
  Find different ways to connect teachers with members of each multiracial student's family, caregivers, or cultural community, to deepen understanding about each student's multiple aspects of identity and culture, beyond formal events.

- **Modify existing curriculum content and instructional strategies.**
  Examine curriculum content and tailor existing or new lessons to address different learning goals, cultures, and topics that enhance understanding about multiracial identity.

- **Appreciate and accommodate similarities and differences among students' cultures.**
  Identify differences among students or cultures in general in a positive manner, which will model and reinforce cross-cultural communication skills, empathy, and respect for differences. Make sure that a tone is set that it is acceptable if a student doesn't know about their own culture; perhaps that is something that can be researched by the class together, or explored at a later time.

❧ Teach children that shifting behaviors according to settings and contexts is a skill.

Normalize the idea that we all behave differently in a variety of settings, with different people, and for different purposes. Teaching students that **code-switching** of behavior, language, and other aspects of communication and interaction is common will help students recognize that behavior in themselves and will help them feel at home when they are naturally interacting in this way.

❧ Be deliberate and intentional in teaching about ethnically, racially, culturally, and socially diverse issues and experiences.

Directly address issues such as cultural diversity, racism, and systemic inequity, which will empower students to build a sense of agency, resilience, and inspiration for social change. It is important to examine the structural and systemic aspects of these forces and outline methods to overcome them and access support, in order to combat stereotype threat or a sense of desperation or isolation by the student.

❧ Embed teaching about ethnic and cultural diversity into rituals, routines, and subjects regularly taught and practiced in schools or in the home.

If teaching about race, ethnicity, cultural diversity, and related issues occurs only at specific times throughout the year (e.g., during Latinx Heritage Month) or in relation to specific events (e.g., Martin Luther King Jr. Day), then it is communicated to children that these topics are less valued and are an "accessory" to the main learning at hand. Instead, establish regular contact with these topics throughout the year and infuse discussions of race and multiple perspectives into ongoing learning and the weekly curriculum.

Dr. Gay suggests many more possibilities for creating a culturally responsive practice. I invite you to examine the other powerful ideas she shares and to think through how to incorporate what was mentioned in this chapter, plus her other suggestions, through the lens of teaching multiracial students. How can we be culturally responsive in our teaching and curriculum planning, to incorporate these viewpoints and to include multiracial children?

ACTION

- **For educators:** Consider how to incorporate these recommendations on culturally responsive teaching into your own curriculum planning and teaching approach.

  - Which of these strategies can be implemented immediately? Which of these approaches will take more time and effort to incorporate, and what can help you achieve this?

  - What hesitation do you have regarding any of these suggested activities? What challenges contribute to this hesitation?

  - Recognize that you are not alone. Foundational work that has already been done is accessible to you. What colleagues, agencies, or organizations can be tapped to support your efforts in culturally responsive teaching for multiracial children? What instructional resources and activities can be found in books, online, or through other methods that can enhance your preparation and planning?

- **For parents and caregivers:** Have a conversation with your child's teacher or school administrator about how positive conceptions of multiracial individuals can be brought up within the classroom through lessons, school activities, curated content, and other learning experiences. You can share the list above and cite Dr. Geneva Gay's work on culturally responsive teaching as the basis for your recommendations.

Why are curriculum and teaching included in this chapter on action and advocacy? This is because it can seem like—and often is—a radical move to reexamine traditional forms of learning and incorporate content on a specific topic or from a new viewpoint. Changes in education to celebrate and include multiracial children are needed and are long overdue.

Continuing Education

While at professional and educational conferences you can look for and attend sessions dedicated to cultivating multiracial identity. There may be sessions, pre-conference workshops, affinity groups, and caucuses dedicated to specific racial demographics, including multiracial identity. If there is not one present, suggest to the conference organizers to create a session track or space for that at their next national or regional event. If you notice that there is a lack of discussion on this topic, consider putting in a proposal for a session or poster session on this topic at the next event, to raise awareness and gather individuals who are like-minded in their passion for this subject.

It can be incredibly frustrating to attend conferences and professional development events that do not have content or spaces dedicated to multiracial identity topics. If you see that being the case, do not be afraid to make noise and draw attention to this fact. Give feedback to the event organizers and also start to connect with other individuals who have similar concerns, to create a joint effort. This advocacy will show that these topics matter and cannot be overlooked or absorbed into conversations about monoracial communities or education in general.

There are a number of conferences that are fantastic resources for exploring race, identity, and education. These are listed in chapter 9. Professional associations of educators, psychologists, counselors, social workers, and those in other specific fields are also good resources to explore for continuing education related to supporting children in their multiracial identity development.

ACTION

- ❧ If you are able to attend professional and educational conferences, locate and attend sessions and gatherings dedicated to multiracial identity and serving multiracial populations.

- ❧ If you observe that conferences and professional development events do not have content or spaces dedicated to exploring multiracial identity, give feedback to the event organizers and request that follow-up actions be taken to address this lack of representation. Connect with others who share similar concerns and are willing to join an effort to create change toward greater inclusion.

Community-Building and Connecting

Does your community have an active gathering of multiracial families or other people interested in educational issues supporting multiracial children? Explore local community resources and see if anything of this nature exists. Perhaps within local nonprofit organizations, there can be a special seminar or other educational event dedicated to this topic. Parent Teacher Associations (PTAs) may be interested in hosting a conversation about the needs of families with multiracial children, or even as a way to introduce families to one another so that they can keep in touch and connect further. Don't be afraid to bring this up as a request and to advocate for this conversation to take place. A single action step can lead to the creation of networks and friendships that can support your child's development beginning from a young age and continuing throughout their lifetime.

Chapter 9 includes a listing of community-based organizations. Two nonprofit organizations that are very active in creating events and dialogue supporting families in person include Multiracial Americans of Southern California (MASC), co-founded in 1986 by Nancy G. Brown and Levonne Gaddy, and Families of Color Seattle (FOCS), founded in 2013 and led by mothers of color. These organizations have wonderful gatherings of committed families and individuals who participate in discussions, social gatherings, and advocacy related to the multiracial community. Many times, the facilitated dialogue and connections with others create a richness of understanding about the multiracial experience, as well as camaraderie around the triumphs and tribulations of raising multiracial children. There are many more national, local, and international organizations dedicated to building communities of multiracial and multiethnic families and children. One other notable movement is Loving Day, founded by Ken Tanabe. Celebrating the anniversary of the *Loving v. Virginia* Supreme Court ruling in favor of interracial marriage on June 12, Loving Day events are held all over the country in the month of June to celebrate interracial love, multiracial families, and unity overall.

Online communities also exist to share positive portrayals of multiracial identity and to prompt us to go further and have deeper conversations about how the diversity of society includes the very important population of multiracial and multiethnic individuals.

Two examples of these online communities include The Mixed Aspect and Mixed Nation, found in various social media channels. There are also other informally organized communities that can be found on Facebook, Meetup, or other online communication avenues, that are accessible to you in your community.

Even if you don't have a preexisting community group or program in your area, another way to build community is to advertise a gathering at your local library or museum around a desired theme. Creating a space and gathering around multiracial topics can serve as a natural introduction to families who are interested in the same topics and issues as you are.

Multiracial children benefit tremendously from being around other multiracial children and families. Adults also find support in sharing stories, resources, and strategies to approach common challenges and may find an ease in being around each other that is a unique experience. This holds true even if the ethnic backgrounds of the individuals participating are not an exact match; what is more important is the spirit of celebrating diversity and coming together in unity regarding multiracial identity and family composition.

ACTION

- Connect with local, regional, or virtual communities focusing on mixed race identity or multiracial families.
- Create social events or other opportunities to gather to meet other families with multiracial children in your neighborhood.

9

Recommended Resources

BEFORE I BECAME A PARENT, I was an organizer and community activist, standing for awareness and educational resources for multiracial and other underrepresented communities. Before that, I was a researcher, investigating intercultural aspects of global encounters and the identity development of multiracial individuals. Prior to that, I was a classroom teacher, engaging students from a variety of different cultural dimensions and needs. And before that, I was a youth, experiencing firsthand what it meant to be of multiethnic heritage and from a multireligious family. These axes of exploration are entry points into the world of multiraciality that I bring to my analysis of what resources would be suitable for multiracial children at various stages in their lives. Moving from a lived experience as a multiethnic person of color to being a parent of multiracial children myself—and now also working as a specialist in diversity, equity, and inclusion—I humbly offer my expertise as a jumping-off point for you to leverage and lean on. There is no need to feel that there is no clear path, or that you are alone in figuring all this out. My wish for all parents, caregivers, and educators is that the contents of this book and this list of resources provide a form of reassurance and stability in this fluid place we are all negotiating with respect to multiracial identity, and that you feel emboldened to take this journey further and define it in your own way.

As many scholars and researchers have noted, an important part of racial identity development is for children to see themselves in the world around them—either in the environment they are living in, or in the things they are exposed to.

During the many years I have been involved in the multiracial community as a community educator and family advocate, I have come across powerful and impactful resources that present issues and raise awareness about multiracial topics in a masterful way.

This chapter highlights my top selections for supplies, toys and games, books on parenting and educating multiracial children, children's books on belonging, diversity, and advocacy and multiracial identity, stories of the multiracial experience, materials that address privilege, race, and racism, conferences, festivals, podcasts and audio clips, art, music, and performing arts, fashion, apparel, and merchandise, multiracial issues–based films and videos, books on multiracial representation, websites, community-based organizations and professional associations, online communities/"social nations," therapy, coaching, and mental health partners, and other resources that can be utilized to bring about awareness of race overall, and community resources to support multiracial identity in children and young adults. This selection is absolutely not a comprehensive list. It is a beginning point, and I am eager to see how you will add to it with your own library of resources and tools!

You can take any of these resources and create an activity, lesson plan, or dialogue around it, in an age-appropriate way that is suitable for your child. You can also experiment with identity exploration in yourself and fellow adults by delving in further, and reflecting on your reactions, as you reimagine your understanding of race with the help of these tools.

I invite you to support the learning, development, and growth of multiracial children by setting the intention to center their experiences and the fluid nature of these identities. It is crucial that we are proactive in establishing the tone of exploration, normalcy, and celebration of being multiracial. Some of these resources will help in that regard.

Just as identity evolves, so does our understanding of it, as well as society's receptiveness to how it is positioned and lived. As we navigate this together, it is important to first and foremost create a place of welcome to the range of ways that multiracial identity can be experienced. And to open up the mindset that a multiracial identity is an option at all.

I leave you with this list of amazing contributions and creations by individuals and groups who are dedicated to envisioning a reality where multiracial individuals belong, thrive, and are seen. Their legacy lives on through us bringing it into our homes, classrooms, and everyday lives. I hope these resources inspire you, as they do for me each day. Seeing this large body of work in appreciation and support of multiracial identity awareness, development, and understanding reaffirms my own efforts. My personal commitment is to continue the work I do to cultivate inclusion for all individuals, and to support underrepresented groups, including multiracial people, as they assume positions of leadership so they in turn can shift narratives, spaces, and dialogue into the overall acceptance and deeper understanding of their lives and lived experiences, in order to expand belonging for all. This is a long-term, broad vision—and I truly believe it is possible. It all first starts with the ability of our multiracial children to be comfortable with themselves. Parents, caregivers, and educators: you are so needed on this deep and long journey to achieve that. Thank you for taking this step to consider your own efforts in advancing understanding about your child's multiracial identity.

Supplies

Lakeshore Learning: People Colors® crayons, colored pencils

SunWorks: multicultural construction paper

Crayola: multicultural crayons, washable markers, colored pencils

Faber-Castell: World Colors EcoPencils

Colorations: multicultural dough

Sax Versatemp: skin-tone tempera paint

My Family Builders™: removable/reusable wall stickers

Lakeshore Learning: families poster pack

Dolls, Toys, and Games

Basket of Babies: plush dolls

My Family Builders™: family diversity blocks, magnetic dolls

Trapolopolis: family dolls, finger puppets (customizable skin colors)

I Never Forget a Face: matching game

Hasbro: Guess Who? board game

Tumi Ishi: wood block set (metaphorical teaching: blocks do not all need to be square or one color)

Little Forest Kids: wooden peg dolls (Waldorf, Inspiring Women lines)

Double Dutch Dolls: multicultural dolls

Barbie Fashionistas™: dolls with different skin tones, hair textures, eye colors, abilities, body shapes

Books on Parenting and Educating Multiracial Children

Multiracial Child Resource Book: Living Complex Identities edited by Maria P. P. Root and Matt Kelley (MAVIN Foundation)

Meeting the Needs of Multiethnic and Multiracial Children in Schools by Francis Wardle and Marta I. Cruz-Janzen

Raising Mixed Race: Multiracial Asian Children in a Post-Racial World by Sharon H. Chang

Raising Biracial Children by Kerry Ann Rockquemore and Tracey A. Laszloffy

Being All of Me: A Handbook for Teachers and Parents of Multiracial, Multiethnic, and Transracially Adopted Children by Farzana Nayani (proceeds benefit the multiracial community)

Mixed-Race Youth and Schooling: The Fifth Minority by Sandra Winn Tutwiler

Does Anybody Else Look Like Me? A Parent's Guide to Raising Multiracial Children by Donna Jackson Nakazawa

To Black Parents Visiting Earth: Raising Black Children in the 21st Century by Janet C. Mendoza Stickmon

Third Culture Kids: Growing Up among Worlds, 3rd ed., by David C. Pollock, Ruth E. Van Reken, and Michael V. Pollock

Multiracial Cultural Attunement by Kelly Faye Jackson and Gina Miranda Samuels

Children's Books: Belonging, Diversity, and Advocacy

I Am Enough by Grace Byers

Whoever You Are by Mem Fox

Ten Little Fingers and Ten Little Toes by Mem Fox

It's Okay to Be Different by Todd Parr

It's a Small World (Disney Parks presents) by Richard M. Sherman and Robert B. Sherman

The Colors of Us by Karen Katz

We're Different, We're the Same (Sesame Street) by Bobbi Jane Kates

The Skin You Live In by Michael Tyler

All Are Welcome by Alexandra Penfold and Suzanne Kaufman

Say Something! by Peter H. Reynolds

A Is for Activist by Innosanto Nagara

All Kinds of Friends by Shelley Rotner and Sheila M. Kelly

What's the Difference? Being Different Is Amazing by Doyin Richards

Kids Like Me: Voices of the Immigrant Experience by Judith M. Blohm and Terri Lapinsky

The Great Big Book of Families by Mary Hoffman

People by Peter Spier

Everyone Matters: A First Look at Respect for Others by Pat Thomas

Should I Make My Curly Hair Straight? by Lesli Mitchell

In Our Mothers' House by Patricia Polacco

All the Colors of the Earth by Sheila Hamanaka

Shades of People by Shelley Rotner and Sheila M. Kelly

The Family Book by Todd Parr

One Love by Cedella Marley

Children's Books: Multiracial

Honeysmoke: A Story of Finding Your Color by Monique Fields

I Am Tan by Michele Rose

black is brown is tan by Arnold Adoff

Mixed Me! by Taye Diggs

I Am Mixed by Garcelle Beauvais and Sebastian A. Jones

MIXED: A Colorful Story by Arree Chung

Amy Hodgepodge (series) by Kim Wayans and Kevin Knotts

How My Parents Learned to Eat by Ina R. Friedman

Mixed Critters: An ABC Book by Jeff Chiba Stearns

All of the Pieces That Make Me, Me by Kathryn Sawh Scott

In a Minute by Tony Bradman and Eileen Browne

Black, White, Just Right! by Marguerite W. Davol

Who's in My Family? All about Our Families by Robie H. Harris

Stories of the Multiracial Experience

When Half Is Whole: Multiethnic Asian American Identities by Stephen Murphy-Shigematsu

What Are You? Voices of Mixed-Race Young People by Pearl Fuyo Gaskins

Half and Half: Writers on Growing Up Biracial and Bicultural edited by Claudine Chiawei O'Hearn

Red and Yellow, Black and Brown: Decentering Whiteness in Mixed Race Studies edited by Joanne L. Rondilla, Rudy P. Guevarra Jr., and Paul Spickard

Being Biracial: Where Our Secret Worlds Collide by Sarah Ratliff and Bryony Sutherland

Hapa Tales and Other Lies: A Mixed Race Memoir about the Hawai'i I Never Knew by Sharon H. Chang

The Girl Who Fell from the Sky by Heidi Durrow

Fade: My Journeys in Multiracial America by Elliott Lewis

Generation Mixed Goes to School (audio clips)

"Being Multiracial in America" (*New York Times* video)

Multiracial American Voices (visual essay by the Pew Research Center, www.pewresearch.org/multiracial-voices/)

Addressing Privilege, Race, and Racism

Why Are All the Black Kids Sitting Together in the Cafeteria? by Beverly D. Tatum

Post Traumatic Slave Syndrome: America's Legacy of Enduring Injury and Healing by Joy DeGruy

Racial Equity Learning Modules (World Trust Educational Services)

So You Want to Talk about Race by Ijeoma Oluo

Cracking the Codes, Healing Justice, and other films by Shakti Butler and World Trust Educational Services

Road to Racial Justice (free "board" game for children and adults) by Kesa Kivel

Some of My Friends Are ...: The Daunting Challenges and Untapped Benefits of Cross-Racial Friendships by Deborah L. Plummer

White Fragility: Why It's So Hard for White People to Talk about Racism by Robin DiAngelo

Uprooting Racism: How White People Can Work for Racial Justice, 4th ed., by Paul Kivel

How to Be an Antiracist by Ibram X. Kendi

The Guide for White Women Who Teach Black Boys edited by Eddie Moore Jr., Ali Michael, and Marguerite W. Penick-Parks

Waking Up White, and Finding Myself in the Story of Race by Debby Irving

The Little Book of Race and Restorative Justice by Fania E. Davis

What Is Systemic Racism? (eight-part video series by Race Forward)

Race Reporting Guide by Race Forward

Showing Up for Racial Justice (SURJ)

Race: The Power of an Illusion (PBS film documentary series and companion website)

Race: Are We So Different? by Alan H. Goodman, Yolanda T. Moses, and Joseph L. Jones (and traveling museum exhibit)

Black History 101 Mobile Museum by Khalid el-Hakim

Teach and Transform by Liz Kleinrock

Conferences

Critical Mixed Race Studies (CMRS)

National Conference on Race and Ethnicity in American Higher Education (NCORE): general sessions and pre-conference workshop

National Association of Independent Schools People of Color Conference (NAIS PoCC): general sessions and multiracial caucus

White Privilege Conference (WPC) and regional events

National Association of Student Personnel Administrators (NASPA): general sessions and MultiRacial Knowledge Community (MRKC)

Hapa Japan Conference

Festivals

Loving Day Festival and regional events

Hapa-palooza

Mixed Remixed Festival

Hapa Japan Festival

Podcasts and Audio Clips

NPR *Code Switch*

Multiracial Family Man: Alex Barnett

What Are You? Mixed Identity Experience

Other: Mixed Race in America: Washington Post

Generation Mixed Goes to School: Center for Communication, Difference, and Equity, University of Washington

Both/And

Critical Mixed Race Studies: 2010 conference sessions

Generation Mixed (series): CBC News, Canada

My American Meltingpot by Lori L. Tharps

Radiant Mix by Hope McGrath

Art, Music, Performing Arts

Laura Kina

Velina Hasu Houston

Jeff Chiba Stearns

Maimouna Youssef

Of Many Colors: Portraits of Multiracial Families by Gigi Kaeser (photography exhibit)

Mixed Blood by CYJO

P.S. ARTS

One Drop of Love

Alien Citizen: An Earth Odyssey

Leila Buck

World Stage Theatre Company, founded by Kelli McLoud-Schingen

Putumayo Kids music collections

Fashion, Apparel, Merchandise

Mixed Up Clothing

Eighth Generation

Mixed Nation

Customize your own on Redbubble, Etsy, Teespring: search using keywords (e.g., multiracial, biracial, mixed)

Beautifully Biracial

Blacklava

Mix-Represented

Multiracial Issues–Based Films and Videos

What Are You? (2019): Richard Pierre

One Big Hapa Family (2010): Jeff Chiba Stearns

Hafu: The Mixed-Race Experience in Japan (2013): Megumi Nishikura and Lara Perez Takagi

Mixed Match (2016): Jeff Chiba Stearns and Athena Asklipiadis

Anomaly (2009): Jessica Chen Drammeh

Loving (2016): Jeff Nichols, with Oscar-nominated performance by Ruth Negga

The Loving Story (2011): documentary by Nancy Buirski

Neither Here Nor There (2011): Ema Ryan Yamazaki

Race in Medicine: A Dangerous Prescription (2012)

What Mixed Race Asians Will Never Tell You: BuzzFeed

The Future of Multiracial Identity: Sylvia Targ's TEDx Talk

#RaceAnd videos: Race Forward

My People Are … Youth Pride in Mixed Heritage film and action booklet: available through SpeakOut—The Institute for Democratic Education and Culture

Books on Multiracial Representation

Mixed: Portraits of Multiracial Kids by Kip Fulbeck

Hāfu2Hāfu by Tetsuro Miyazaki

Part Asian, 100% Hapa by Kip Fulbeck

Of Many Colors: Portraits of Multiracial Families by Gigi Kaeser

Mixed Blood by CYJO

Blended Nation: Portraits and Interviews of Mixed-Race America by Mike Tauber and Pamela Singh

Critical Mixed Race Studies

Mixed Race Studies: scholarly perspectives on the mixed race experience, www.mixedracestudies.org

Critical Mixed Race Studies, *Journal of Critical Mixed Race Studies,* https://criticalmixedracestudies.com

Interactive

"How Census Race Categories Have Changed Over Time," Pew Research Center

The Legal Map for Interracial Relationships (1662–1967) (map showing how interracial marriage was restricted by US state, over time), Loving Day, www.lovingday.org/legal-map

Race, www.understandingrace.org

Community-Based Organizations and Professional Associations

Multiracial Americans of Southern California (MASC)

Loving Day

Biracial Family Network (BFN)

Mixed Roots Stories

Mixed in the Six

Families of Color Seattle (FOCS) (multiracial families parent groups)

Mixed Roots Japan

Mixed in Canada

Jewish Multiracial Network

Project RACE

American College Personnel Association (ACPA) Multiracial Network (MRN)

UCLA Mixed Alumni Association

Association for Asian American Studies (AAAS), Mixed Race section

Mixed Marrow

On-campus student-led multiracial organizations at colleges and universities

Online Communities/ "Social Nations"

Biracial Family Network (BFN)

Mixed Nation

The Mixed Aspect

Subtle Mixed Traits

Swirl, Inc.

Multiracial Media

Muslim Christian Interfaith Families

Mixed Race Babies

Mixed Race Children

Our Grams Place (grandparents of multiracial grandchildren)

Culturas

Therapy, Coaching, Mental Health, Relationships, Healing

Dr. Jennifer Noble, licensed psychologist and therapist for mixed race teens and their parents

Lisa Williamson Rosenberg, psychotherapist/LCSW

Dr. Allison Briscoe-Smith, psychologist

The Swirl Method by Carmen White Janak and Timothy Janak

Tamara Thorpe, the Millennials Mentor

Dr. Jennifer Lisa Vest, medical intuitive

Heather Rebecca Wilson, transformational coach

Ridvan Foxhall, occupational therapist, parent educator, youth leadership facilitator

Jewel Love, MA, LMFT, therapist and facilitator: Black Executive Men, Interracial Couples Counseling

Multiracial Family and Couples Project, Ackerman Institute for the Family

American Association for Marriage and Family Therapy (AAMFT)

My Grandmother's Hands: Racialized Trauma and the Pathway to Mending Our Hearts and Bodies by Resmaa Menakem

The Racial Healing Handbook: Practical Activities to Help You Challenge Privilege, Confront Systemic Racism & Engage in Collective Healing by Anneliese A. Singh

The Inner Work of Racial Justice: Healing Ourselves and Transforming Our Communities through Mindfulness by Rhonda V. Magee

A

Glossary

THIS GLOSSARY HAS been compiled from a variety of sources and is meant to be a reference for the reader to support understanding of the topics in this book, and to help provide a common language to enhance discussion and exploration. The full list of references can be found in the endnotes section of this book.

Affinity Group A group of people having a common interest or goal or acting together for a specific purpose. In institutional settings, this is a group that gathers and organizes around a common demographic characteristic such as race, gender, or other identity trait, in order to create community.

Ally Someone who makes the commitment and effort to recognize their privilege (based on gender, class, race, sexual identity, etc.) and work in solidarity with oppressed groups in the struggle for justice. Allies understand that it is in their own interest to end all forms of oppression, even those from which they may benefit in concrete ways.

Allies commit to reducing their own complicity or collusion in oppression of those groups and invest in strengthening their own knowledge and awareness of oppression.

Anti-Multiracial Bias Bias against multiracial individuals and groups. This term has been used in describing bias in civil rights cases and within hate-crime statistics.

BIPOC: Black, Indigenous, and Other People of Color A term emphasizing authentic and lasting solidarity among Black, Indigenous, and other People of Color that exists to highlight the unique relationship that Indigenous and Black (African American) people have to Whiteness and White supremacy, in order to undo Native invisibility and anti-Blackness.

Biracial Identity of two different races.

Code-switch/Code-switching Originally referring to the switching from the linguistic system of one language or dialect to that of another, code-switching in the cultural or racial context refers to intentionally adapting and moving between culturally ingrained systems of behavior and communication styles relevant to the situation at hand.

Colonial Mentality An internalized attitude of inferiority within cultural and ethnic minorities that is a result of extensive oppression related to colonialism, including the belief that the cultural values of the colonizer are inherently superior.

Colonialism Colonization can be defined as some form of invasion, dispossession, and subjugation of a people. The invasion need not be military; it can begin—or continue—as geographic intrusion in the form of agricultural, urban, or industrial encroachments. The result of such incursion is the dispossession of vast amounts of lands from the original inhabitants. This is often legalized after the fact. The long-term result of such massive dispossession is institutionalized inequality. The colonizer/colonized relationship is by nature an unequal one that benefits the colonizer at the expense of the colonized.

Color-blind In the context of racial dynamics, not influenced by differences of race; free from racial prejudice.

Colorism A system of hierarchy within communities that favors lighter skin and proximity to Whiteness and affords privileges and preferences to individuals with lighter skin and other physical characteristics (hair texture, facial features, etc.) that approximate Whiteness.

Covering (as in identity) Identity covering is the act of concealing something about one's self to lessen attention to a given characteristic, in order to fit in with the surrounding group. This includes downplaying aspects of your identity, such as race, religion, gender, disability, or sexual orientation, to avoid feelings of anxiety, frustration, fear, or lack of belonging.

Cultural Appropriation Theft of cultural elements for one's own use, commodification, or profit—including symbols, art, language, customs, etc.—often without understanding, acknowledgment of, or respect for its value in the original culture. It results from the assumption of a dominant culture's right to take other cultural elements.

Culture A social system of meaning and custom that is developed by a group of people to assure its adaptation and survival. These groups are distinguished by a set of unspoken rules that shape values, beliefs, habits, patterns of thinking, behaviors, and styles of communication.

Discrimination The unequal treatment of members of various groups based on race, gender, social class, sexual orientation, physical ability, religion, and other categories.

In the United States, the law makes it illegal to discriminate against someone on the basis of race, color, religion, national origin, or sex. The law also makes it illegal to retaliate against a person because the person complained about discrimination, filed a charge of discrimination, or participated in an employment discrimination investigation or lawsuit. The law also requires that employers reasonably accommodate applicants' and employees' sincerely held religious practices, unless doing so would impose an undue hardship on the operation of the employer's business.

Diversity Diversity includes all the ways in which people differ, and it encompasses all the different characteristics that make one individual or group different from another. It is all-inclusive and recognizes everyone and every group as part of the diversity that should be valued. A broad definition includes not only race, ethnicity, and gender—the groups that most often come to mind when the term "diversity" is used—but also age, national origin, religion, disability, sexual orientation, socioeconomic status, education, marital status, language, and physical appearance. It also involves different ideas, perspectives, and values.

Employee Resource Group (ERG) An affinity group created at the workplace with a defined purpose and an organizational process, and organized around and in service of a particular demographic category or identity characteristic.

Equity Acknowledgment, treatment, actions, and opportunity to address that many groups in society have not always been given equal treatment and are frequently made to feel inferior and oppressed. This can be in the form of education, awareness-building around specific issues, and special programs and benefits for those who have been discriminated against and are in need of opportunity.

Ethnicity A social construct that divides people into smaller social groups based on characteristics such as shared sense of group membership, values, behavioral patterns, language, political and economic interests, history, and ancestral geographic base. Members of the group share common cultural traits such as religion and dress. Examples of different ethnic groups are Cape Verdean, Haitian, African American (Black); Chinese, Korean, Vietnamese (Asian); Cherokee, Mohawk, Navaho (Native American); Cuban, Mexican, Puerto Rican (Latinx); and Polish, Irish, Swedish (White).

Exceptionalism Highlighting the successes of an individual from a marginalized group to counter their associations with the negative stereotypes of the group. However, it actually reinforces the stereotype, because it focuses on the individual achievement and superiority of a single person, rather than the systemic inequity and bias that has created the stereotype in the first place.

Filipinx A term indicating heritage from the Philippines that is inclusive of gender nonconfirming individuals. Utilizing the terms Filipino/Filipina or even Filipin@ indicates a gender binary that is not inclusive of the entire spectrum of gender identity, including those who identify as genderqueer. Note: there is a wide range of awareness, acceptance, and usage of this term. In addition to gender identity, differences in opinion around this term can be due to location (e.g., United States, the Philippines, or other parts of the world) or generation (the older generation may be unaware of or uncomfortable with this term).

Forced Choice Originally referring to a specific format for response options in survey questionnaires, a "forced-choice" experience is a scenario or situation where an individual must choose from a fixed number of options, thereby limiting freedom of will, decision, and expression.

Hapa Being of mixed ethnic heritage (this term originated in Hawai'i meaning "part"). In some locales, the term is often used to indicate mixed Asian heritage. Note: this term is contested as it is embraced by some members of the community as an endearing term that wholly describes their identity and connection to the multiracial community, whereas it is also experienced negatively as a culturally appropriated term that marginalizes the Native Hawaiian community.

Horizontal Racism Results in targeted racial groups believing, acting on, or enforcing the dominant (White) system of racial discrimination and oppression. Horizontal racism can occur between members of the same racial group (e.g., an Asian person telling another Asian wearing a sari to "dress like an American"; a Latinx person telling another Latinx person to stop speaking Spanish) or between members of different, targeted racial groups (e.g., Latinx people believing stereotypes about Native Americans; Black individuals not wanting Asians to move into a predominantly Black neighborhood).

Identity Autonomy The freedom and self-governance to select and live out a chosen identity.

Implicit Bias Also known as unconscious or hidden bias, implicit biases are negative associations that people unknowingly hold. They are expressed automatically, without conscious awareness. Many studies have indicated that implicit biases affect individuals' attitudes and actions, thus creating real-world implications, even though individuals may not even be aware that those biases exist within themselves. Notably, implicit biases have been shown to trump individuals' stated commitments to equality and fairness, thereby producing behavior that diverges from the explicit attitudes that many people profess. The Implicit Association Test (IAT) is often used to measure implicit biases with regard to race, gender, sexual orientation, age, religion, and other topics.

Imposter Syndrome (regarding race, see "Racial Imposter Syndrome") A pattern of behavior where people exhibit doubt and have a persistent, often internalized fear of being exposed as a fraud. This term is broadly understood in connection with doubt in one's accomplishments.

Inclusion Authentically bringing traditionally excluded individuals and/or groups into processes, activities, and decision/policy making in a way that shares power.

Indigenous Indigenous populations are composed of the existing descendants of the peoples who inhabited the present territory of a country wholly or partially at the time when persons of a different culture or ethnic origin arrived there from other parts of the world, overcame them, by conquest, settlement, or other means, and reduced them to a nondominant or colonial condition; who today live more in conformity with their particular social, economic, and cultural customs and traditions than with the institutions of the country of which they now form a part, under a state structure that incorporates mainly national, social, and cultural characteristics of other segments of the population that are predominant (examples: Maori in territory now defined as New Zealand; Mexicans and Native American tribes in territory now defined as the United States).

Inequity The experience and understanding that many groups in society have not always been given equal treatment and are frequently made to feel inferior and oppressed.

Intent versus Impact The idea that even though a person may have positive intentions, their actions or behaviors can still result in a negative impact. Also important is acknowledging that the depth and negative experience of the impact on a recipient of an interaction should not be dismissed just because there was positive intent on the part of the doer in the interaction.

Intercultural Occurring between or involving two or more cultures.

Internalized Oppression When members of a target group believe, act on, or enforce the dominant system of beliefs about themselves and members of their own group. For example, internalized sexism involves women applying principles of male dominance and oppression to themselves and/or other women.

Interracial Relationship in which there are partners of different races; often used to describe couples and unions (e.g., interracial marriage).

Intersectionality An approach largely advanced by women of color, arguing that classifications such as gender, race, and class cannot be examined in isolation from one another, and can result in compounded oppression. The classifications interact and intersect in individuals' lives, in society, and in social systems.

LGBTQ+ Lesbian, gay, bisexual, transgender, and queer/questioning (one's sexual or gender identity), with the plus indicating other identities on the gender identity spectrum (such as two spirit, intersex, asexual, and more).

Marginalization Treatment of a person, group, or concept as insignificant or peripheral; relegation to an unimportant or powerless position within a society or group.

Microaggressions Subtle, brief, commonplace, and often unconscious messages that single out, ignore, or otherwise discount individuals or groups based on aspects of their social identities (e.g., race, gender, age).

Mixed Race Identity referring to the mixing of two or more races.

Monoracial Identity of one race.

Monoracism The systemic privileging of things, people, and practices that are racialized as "single race" and/or "racially pure" (e.g., monoracial) and the oppression of things, people, and practices that are racialized as being more than one race (e.g., multiracial, mixed race, multiethnic, etc.).

Mulatto A mixed race person of Black and White parentage. Note: this term has a negative connotation and is considered to be derogatory and offensive.

Multiethnic Identity of two or more ethnicities.

Multiracial Identity of two or more races.

Multiracial Identity Quagmire The space and experience where a multiracial person feels that they do not belong anywhere, due to not being accepted or not having the traits and behaviors to fully fit in. A complete lack of belonging or inclusion due to one's multiracial identity.

Multiracial Microaggressions Microaggressions that impact and marginalize multiracial individuals through the process of exclusion and isolation, exoticization and objectification, assumption of a monoracial identity, denial of a multiracial identity, and pathologizing of multiracial identity and experiences.

Multiracial Positive Open and positive conceptions of a multiracial identity. Similar to "body positive" or "sex positive."

Multiracial Positivity A social movement that promotes a positive sense of self around multiracial identity. Similar to "body positivity."

Nationality One's country of origin or citizenship.

Object Permanence The understanding that objects continue to exist even when they cannot be perceived (seen, heard, touched, smelled, tasted, or sensed in any way). Usually associated with children's cognitive development.

Octoroon A term used to describe a person with "one-eighth Black parentage." Since this term is a label that was historically used to uphold the "one-drop rule" and assignment to a subordinate group, this term has a negative connotation.

People of Color (POC) A term born out of the anti-racism movement to describe non-White individuals. The term is meant to be inclusive among non-White groups, emphasizing common experiences of racism and oppression, and resistance to racism and oppression.

Performing (as in "performing" identity) A conscious effort or action to present one's identity in a given way within social interactions. The performance of racial identity can take place through how one's physical appearance is presented (e.g., hairstyles, clothing, etc.), communication (e.g., utilizing in-group lingo or jargon or accents), behaviors (e.g., choice of social activities or friend groups), and other methods of expression.

Phenotype The physical appearance of a person and physical characteristics including skin color, facial features, hair texture, and eye shape.

Post-racial Denoting or relating to a period or society in which racial prejudice and discrimination no longer exist. Having overcome or moved beyond racism; having reached a stage or time at which racial prejudice no longer exists or is no longer a major social problem.

Privilege Unearned social power accorded by the formal and informal institutions of society to all members of a dominant group (e.g., White privilege, male privilege, etc.). Systemic favoring, enriching, valuing, validating, and including of certain social identities over others. Privilege is usually invisible to those who have it because we're taught not to see it, but nevertheless it puts them at an advantage over those who do not have it. Individuals cannot "opt out" of systems of privilege; these systems are inherent to the society in which we live.

Quadroon A term used to describe a person with "one-fourth Black parentage." Since this term is a label that was historically used to uphold the "one-drop rule" and assignment to a subordinate group, this term has a negative connotation.

Race There is no biological basis for racial categories, and genetic research has shown more within-group variations than between-group variations. Races are socially and politically constructed categories that others have assigned on the basis of physical characteristics, such as skin color or hair type. Although race is a social construction, the impact of race is real, as perceptions of race influence our beliefs, stereotypes, economic opportunities, and everyday experiences.

Racial Equity Racial equity is the condition that would be achieved if one's racial identity no longer predicted, in a statistical sense, how one fares. When we use the term, we are thinking about racial equity as one part of racial justice, and thus we also include work to address root causes of inequities, not just their manifestation. This includes elimination of policies, practices, attitudes, and cultural messages that reinforce differential outcomes by race or fail to eliminate them.

Racial Imposter Syndrome Imposter syndrome is a term referring to a pattern of behavior where people exhibit doubt and have a persistent, often internalized fear of being exposed as a fraud. This term is broadly understood in connection with doubt in one's accomplishments. However, "racial imposter syndrome" relates to "feeling 'fake' or inauthentic in some part of their racial or ethnic heritage."

Racial Justice Racial justice is defined as the proactive reinforcement of policies, practices, attitudes, and actions that produce equitable power, access, opportunities, treatment, impacts, and outcomes for all.

Racial Legitimacy Needing to prove one's belonging within a racial group.

Racism: Individual Individual racism refers to the beliefs, attitudes, and actions of individuals that support or perpetuate racism. Individual racism can be deliberate, or the individual may act to perpetuate or support racism without knowing that is what they are doing.

Examples:

- Telling a racist joke, using a racial epithet, or believing in the inherent superiority of White individuals over other groups

- Avoiding People of Color whom you do not know personally, but not White individuals whom you do not know personally (e.g., White people crossing the street to avoid a group of Latinx young people; clutching their purses when they are with African American individuals in an elevator; or not hiring a Person of Color because "something doesn't feel right")

- Accepting things as they are (a form of collusion)

Racism: Institutional Institutional racism refers specifically to the ways in which institutional policies and practices create different outcomes for different racial groups. The institutional policies may never mention any racial group, but their effect is to create advantages for White individuals (or those approximating Whiteness) and oppression and disadvantages for people from groups classified as People of Color.

Examples:

- ෂ Government policies that explicitly restrict the ability of people to get loans to buy homes or improve their homes in neighborhoods with high concentrations of African Americans (also known as "redlining")

- ෂ City sanitation department policies that concentrate trash transfer stations and other environmental hazards disproportionately in communities of color

Resilience The capacity or ability to recover quickly from difficulties or adjust easily to misfortune or change.

Social Justice Refers to human rights and justice in terms of the distribution of wealth, opportunities, and privileges within a society.

Stereotype An overgeneralization based on race, gender, sexual orientation, class, ability, age, and other characteristics that is widely believed about an entire group of people. Stereotypes are impervious to evidence and contrary argument.

Stereotype Threat Refers to being at risk of confirming, as a self-characteristic, a negative stereotype about one's social group.

Systemic Oppression Systemic devaluing, undermining, marginalizing, and disadvantaging of certain social identities in contrast to the privileged norm; when some people are denied something of value, while others have ready access.

Third Culture Kid (TCK) Children who are raised in a culture other than their parents' culture or passport country, for a significant part of their early development.

Transracial Adoptee Identity of being adopted by a family of a different race than the adoptee.

Unconscious Bias See "Implicit Bias."

White Privilege Refers to the unquestioned and unearned set of advantages, entitlements, benefits, and choices bestowed on people solely because they are White. Generally, White people who experience such privilege do so without being conscious of it.

White Supremacy The systemic dominance of White culture based on the assumption or theory that Whites are inherently superior to all other races and should be in power and control.

B

Social Justice Standards: Grade-Level Outcomes

FROM THE TEACHING TOLERANCE publication "Social Justice Standards: A Professional Development Facilitator Guide" (2018).[1]

Reprinted with permission of Teaching Tolerance, a project of the Southern Poverty Law Center. More information can be found about this and other resources at www.tolerance.org.

K–2 Grade-Level Outcomes

ANCHOR STANDARD	CODE	GRADE-LEVEL OUTCOME
Identity 1	ID.K-2.1	I know and like who I am and can talk about my family and myself and name some of my group identities.
Identity 2	ID.K-2.2	I can talk about interesting and healthy ways that some people who share my group identities live their lives.
Identity 3	ID.K-2.3	I know that all my group identities are part of me—but that I am always ALL me.
Identity 4	ID.K-2.4	I can feel good about myself without being mean or making other people feel bad.
Identity 5	ID.K-2.5	I see that the way my family and I do things is both the same as and different from how other people do things, and I am interested in both.
Diversity 6	DI.K-2.6	I like being around people who are like me and different from me, and I can be friendly to everyone.
Diversity 7	DI.K-2.7	I can describe some ways that I am similar to and different from people who share my identities and those who have other identities.
Diversity 8	DI.K-2.8	I want to know about other people and how our lives and experiences are the same and different.
Diversity 9	DI.K-2.9	I know everyone has feelings, and I want to get along with people who are similar to and different from me.
Diversity 10	DI.K-2.10	I find it interesting that groups of people believe different things and live their daily lives in different ways.
Justice 11	JU.K-2.11	I know my friends have many identities, but they are always still just themselves.
Justice 12	JU.K-2.12	I know when people are treated unfairly.

ANCHOR STANDARD	CODE	GRADE-LEVEL OUTCOME
Justice 13	JU.K-2.13	I know some true stories about how people have been treated badly because of their group identities, and I don't like it.
Justice 14	JU.K-2.14	I know life is easier for some people and harder for others and the reasons for that are not always fair.
Justice 15	JU.K-2.15	I know about people who helped stop unfairness and worked to make life better for many people.
Action 16	AC.K-2.16	I care about those who are treated unfairly.
Action 17	AC.K-2.17	I can and will do something when I see unfairness—this includes telling an adult.
Action 18	AC.K-2.18	I will say something or tell an adult if someone is being hurtful, and will do my part to be kind even if I don't like something they say or do.
Action 19	AC.K-2.19	I will speak up or do something if people are being unfair, even if my friends do not.
Action 20	AC.K-2.20	I will join with classmates to make our classroom fair for everyone.

3–5 Grade-Level Outcomes

ANCHOR STANDARD	CODE	GRADE-LEVEL OUTCOME
Identity 1	ID.3-5.1	I know and like who I am and can talk about my family and myself and describe our various group identities.
Identity 2	ID.3-5.2	I know about my family history and culture and about current and past contributions of people in my main identity groups.
Identity 3	ID.3-5.3	I know that all my group identities are a part of who I am, but none of them fully describes me and this is true for other people too.

ANCHOR STANDARD	CODE	GRADE-LEVEL OUTCOME
Identity 4	ID.3-5.4	I can feel good about my identity without making someone else feel badly about who they are.
Identity 5	ID.3-5.5	I know my family and I do things the same as and different from other people and groups, and I know how to use what I learn from home, school, and other places that matter to me.
Diversity 6	DI.3-5.6	I like knowing people who are like me and different from me, and I treat each person with respect.
Diversity 7	DI.3-5.7	I have accurate, respectful words to describe how similar I am to and different from people who share my identities and those who have other identities.
Diversity 8	DI.3-5.8	I want to know more about other people's lives and experiences, and I know how to ask questions respectfully and listen carefully and non-judgmentally.
Diversity 9	DI.3-5.9	I feel connected to other people and know how to talk, work, and play with others even when we are different or when we disagree.
Diversity 10	DI.3-5.10	I know that the way groups of people are treated today, and the way they have been treated in the past, is a part of what makes them who they are.
Justice 11	JU.3-5.11	I try and get to know people as individuals because I know it is unfair to think all people in a shared identity group are the same.
Justice 12	JU.3-5.12	I know when people are treated unfairly, and I can give examples of prejudice words, pictures and rules.
Justice 13	JU.3-5.13	I know that words, behaviors, rules and laws that treat people unfairly based on their group identities cause real harm.

ANCHOR STANDARD	CODE	GRADE-LEVEL OUTCOME
Justice 14	JU.3-5.14	I know that life is easier for some people and harder for others based on who they are and where they were born.
Justice 15	JU.3-5.15	I know about the actions of people and groups who have worked throughout history to bring more justice and fairness to the world.
Action 16	AC.3-5.16	I pay attention to how people (including myself) are treated, and I try to treat others how I like to be treated.
Action 17	AC.3-5.17	I know it's important for me to stand up for myself and for others, and I know how to get help if I need ideas on how to do this.
Action 18	AC.3-5.18	I know some ways to interfere if someone is being hurtful or unfair, and will do my part to show respect even if I disagree with someone's words or behavior.
Action 19	AC.3-5.19	I will speak up or do something when I see unfairness, and I will not let others convince me to go along with injustice.
Action 20	AC.3-5.20	I will work with my friends and family to make our school and community fair for everyone, and we will work hard and cooperate in order to achieve our goals.

6–8 Grade-Level Outcomes

ANCHOR STANDARD	CODE	GRADE-LEVEL OUTCOME
Identity 1	ID.6-8.1	I know and like who I am and can talk about my family and myself and describe our various group identities.
Identity 2	ID.6-8.2	I know about my family history and culture and how I am connected to the collective history and culture of other people in my identity groups.

ANCHOR STANDARD	CODE	GRADE-LEVEL OUTCOME
Identity 3	ID.6-8.3	I know that overlapping identities combine to make me who I am and that none of my group identities on their own fully defines me or any other person.
Identity 4	ID.6-8.4	I feel good about my many identities and know they don't make me better than people with other identities.
Identity 5	ID.6-8.5	I know there are similarities and differences between my home culture and the other environments and cultures I encounter, and I can be myself in a diversity of settings.
Diversity 6	DI.6-8.6	I interact with people who are similar to and different from me, and I show respect to all people.
Diversity 7	DI.6-8.7	I can accurately and respectfully describe ways that people (including myself) are similar to and different from each other and others in their identity groups.
Diversity 8	DI.6-8.8	I am curious and want to know more about other people's histories and lived experiences, and I ask questions respectfully and listen carefully and non-judgmentally.
Diversity 9	DI.6-8.9	I know I am connected to other people and can relate to them even when we are different or when we disagree.
Diversity 10	DI.6-8.10	I can explain how the way groups of people are treated today, and the way they have been treated in the past, shapes their group identity and culture.
Justice 11	JU.6-8.11	I relate to people as individuals and not representatives of groups, and I can name some common stereotypes I observe people using.

ANCHOR STANDARD	CODE	GRADE-LEVEL OUTCOME
Justice 12	JU.6-8.12	I can recognize and describe unfairness and injustice in many forms including attitudes, speech, behaviors, practices and laws.
Justice 13	JU.6-8.13	I am aware that biased words and behaviors and unjust practices, laws and institutions limit the rights and freedoms of people based on their identity groups.
Justice 14	JU.6-8.14	I know that all people (including myself) have certain advantages and disadvantages in society based on who they are and where they were born.
Justice 15	JU.6-8.15	I know about some of the people, groups and events in social justice history and about the beliefs and ideas that influenced them.
Action 16	AC.6-8.16	I am concerned about how people (including myself) are treated and feel for people when they are excluded or mistreated because of their identities.
Action 17	AC.6-8.17	I know how to stand up for myself and for others when faced with exclusion, prejudice, and injustice.
Action 18	AC.6-8.18	I can respectfully tell someone when [their] words or actions are biased or hurtful.
Action 19	AC.6-8.19	I will speak up or take action when I see unfairness, even if those around me do not, and I will not let others convince me to go along with injustice.
Action 20	AC.6-8.20	I will work with my friends, family and community members to make our world fairer for everyone, and we will plan and coordinate our actions in order to achieve our goals.

9–12 Grade-Level Outcomes

ANCHOR STANDARD	CODE	GRADE-LEVEL OUTCOME
Identity 1	ID.9-12.1	I have a positive view of myself, including an awareness of and comfort with my membership in multiple groups in society.
Identity 2	ID.9-12.2	I know my family history and cultural background and can describe how my own identity is informed and shaped by my membership in multiple identity groups.
Identity 3	ID.9-12.3	I know that all my group identities and the intersection of those identities create unique aspects of who I am and that this is true for other people too.
Identity 4	ID.9-12.4	I express pride and confidence in my identity without perceiving or treating anyone else as inferior.
Identity 5	ID.9-12.5	I recognize the traits of the dominant culture, my home culture and other cultures, and I am conscious of how I express my identity as I move between those spaces.
Diversity 6	DI.9-12.6	I interact comfortably and respectfully with all people, whether they are similar to or different from me.
Diversity 7	DI.9-12.7	I have the language and knowledge to accurately and respectfully describe how people (including myself) are both similar to and different from each other and others in their identity groups.
Diversity 8	DI.9-12.8	I respectfully express curiosity about the history and lived experiences of others and exchange ideas and beliefs in an open-minded way.
Diversity 9	DI.9-12.9	I relate to and build connections with other people by showing them empathy, respect and understanding, regardless of our similarities or differences.

ANCHOR STANDARD	CODE	GRADE-LEVEL OUTCOME
Diversity 10	DI.9-12.10	I understand that diversity includes the impact of unequal power relations on the development of group identities and cultures.
Justice 11	JU.9-12.11	I relate to all people as individuals rather than representatives of groups and can identify common stereotypes when I see or hear them.
Justice 12	JU.9-12.12	I can recognize, describe and distinguish unfairness and injustice at different levels of society.
Justice 13	JU.9-12.13	I can explain the short and long-term impact of biased words and behaviors and unjust practices, laws and institutions that limit the rights and freedoms of people based on their identity groups.
Justice 14	JU.9-12.14	I am aware of the advantages and disadvantages I have in society because of my membership in different identity groups, and I know how this has affected my life.
Justice 15	JU.9-12.15	I can identify figures, groups, events and a variety of strategies and philosophies relevant to the history of social justice around the world.
Action 16	AC.9-12.16	I express empathy when people are excluded or mistreated because of their identities and concern when I personally experience bias.
Action 17	AC.9-12.17	I take responsibility for standing up to exclusion, prejudice and injustice.
Action 18	AC.9-12.18	I have the courage to speak up to people when their words, actions or views are biased or hurtful, and I will communicate with respect even when we disagree.
Action 19	AC.9-12.19	I stand up to exclusion, prejudice and discrimination, even when it's not popular or easy or when no one else does.

ANCHOR STANDARD	CODE	GRADE-LEVEL OUTCOME
Action 20	AC.9-12.20	I will join with diverse people to plan and carry out collective action against exclusion, prejudice and discrimination, and we will be thoughtful and creative in our actions in order to achieve our goals.

Lesson Plans

IN PREPARATION for each lesson, please review related terminology in the glossary in Appendix A.

For more lesson plan support and ideas, and updates on future resources, please visit www.farzananayani.com.

Grade Level: *K–2, 3–5*

Title: *"Our Unique Families"*

Subjects: *Language Arts, Social Studies, Current Events*

Education Standards Addressed: ID.K-2.1 to ID.K-2.10, JU.K-2.11, ID.3-5.1 to ID.3-5.10, AC.3-5.20

Learning Objectives

Exposing children to the variety of different families that exist, and fostering appreciation for the different types of families found within one's own life and community, and the world overall.

Resources

The Family Book by Todd Parr (2003)

Who's in My Family? All about Our Families by Robie H. Harris (2012)

The Great Big Book of Families by Mary Hoffman (2010)

Activities

1. Read one of the books listed above. Have a discussion about the types of families that are found. Include guiding questions in the discussion such as

    "How are families different from one another?"

    "Who is in your family? What does your family look like?"

    "How do family members look like us or are different from us?"

    It is important to explain that families do not have to be by birth; they can include caregivers, foster parents, or adoptive parents—they are all family to us.

2. Project. Ask students to "Find out from your family members what their favorite things are! Share with us what makes them unique!" Examples of ideas could be sports, foods, hobbies. For the uniqueness question, model positively that having family members from different cultures may make a family unique! Fill out a worksheet to capture this information, and to be used as a prompt.

   Example of worksheet prompts could be: "___(name)___ is in my family. ___(name)___ is my ___(relationship to child)___. ___(name)___'s favorite things are _____ because _____. Something unique about my family is _____."

   Use this information to create a poem about your family. Decorate the poem by drawing pictures of your family members' favorite things.

3. Poetry Showcase. After writing, editing, and publishing the poems, the children share them with the rest of the class or with their family members.

Extension: Ancestors / Family Lineage

1. Think about family members who are no longer with us. Explain the concept of an *ofrenda* and how it is a part of Día de Muertos and Latinx heritage. Explore with the children: If we created an ofrenda for your family members, what could we put on the ofrenda? Do you have other ways of remembering relatives and ancestors?

2. Have the children create a diorama of their ofrenda, including photos or mementos from their family.

   This activity helps create a tie to a child's ancestors and family lineage, and brings in components of culture that can connect with the child further. Note that there should be an explanation and creative expansion of this activity for adopted or foster children to include individuals who are not their immediate birth relatives, or a commemoration of their general culture and heritage, to make sure they feel included and not left out through this activity.

Extension: Multiracial and Global Families

1. With the class (or with your child), read the book *How My Parents Learned to Eat* by Ina R. Friedman (1984).

2. Discuss with the child: What do you use to eat at home? Do you use a fork and knife? Fork and spoon? Chopsticks? Your hands? Do you use more than one thing?

   Discuss how different cultures eat using different utensils or their hands and may not use a plate, but could use a banana leaf or a paper wrapper, for instance. Expand the conversations about families to different families around the world, and how multiracial and other families could have a combination of these things present within one family.

Grade Level: *6–8, 9–12*

Title: *"Separate and Mixed"*

Subjects: *Social Studies, History, Language Arts, Math*

Education Standards Addressed: This activity can potentially address all standards for grades 6–8 and grades 9–12: ID.6-8.1 through ID.6-8.5, DI.6-8.6 through DI.6-8.10, JU.6-8.11 through JU.6-8.15, AC.6-8.16 through AC.6-8.20, ID.9-12.1 through ID.9-12.5, DI.9-12.6 through DI.9-12.10, JU.9-12.11 through JU.9-12.15, AC.9-12.16 through AC.9-12.20

Learning Objectives

Exploring concepts of identity, social justice, segregation, marginalization, privilege, inclusion, belonging, intersectionality, and multiracial community-building.

Resources

MIXED: A Colorful Story by Arree Chung (2018)

Being All of Me: A Handbook for Teachers and Parents of Multiracial, Multiethnic, and Transracially Adopted Children by Farzana Nayani (2017)

Activities

1. Read the book *MIXED: A Colorful Story* with the class.

2. Ask the group:

   What could these colors represent? How do these colors interact with or avoid one another?

   Who has more power or freedom in the story?

   When have you felt a part of one group but not another?

When have you felt a part of more than one group at the same time?

How does this describe multiracial identity in particular?

3. Activity. Ask each child to draw a Venn diagram of the different groups that the child is a part of, and use different colors to illustrate how they overlap and intersect. What do the "mixed" areas represent to the child?

4. Invite children to compare their Venn diagrams with a classmate or neighbor. Ask the following and other guiding questions: "How are the Venn diagrams the same or different? What do you notice?"

5. Share information about how in history and in the current day, there are both aspects of separation and coming together of cultures and communities. Introduce terminology related to segregation, human rights, marginalization, privilege, etc. Ask children to reflect on this story as a metaphor for cultural differences (including race, gender, gender identity, sexual orientation, religion, ability, and more) and how these differences are favored or are disadvantaged.

6. Debrief the entire activity with the children. Share the poem from *Being All of Me* called "Colors" about being a part of more than one community and creating your own.

Extension: Multiracial or Blended Culture

Create a poem similar to "Colors" and using a few of the aspects of identity and community that were listed on the Venn diagram. Express what it is like to be a part of more than one community at the same time, and how these communities come together to make a child's identity.

Note: It is especially important that this lesson and activities are done after there has been an effort to foster a culture of inclusion, respect, and trust in the school or family environment of the child.

For further reading about the intersectionality of being multiracial and a global/third culture kid, watch the solo show *Alien Citizen: An Earth Odyssey* by Elizabeth Liang (available on DVD).

For more background on third culture kids and blended culture:

Cultural Detective Blended Culture (available online)

Third Culture Kids: Growing Up among Worlds, 3rd ed., by David C. Pollock, Ruth E. Van Reken, and Michael V. Pollock (2017)

Grade Level: *9–12*

Title: *"Loving Day Lives"*

Subjects: *History, Social Studies, Current Events, Language Arts*

Education Standards Addressed: *I*D.9-12.12, DI.9-12.10, JU.9-12.12, JU.9-12.13, JU.9-12.15, AC.9-12.16, AC.9-12.17

Learning Objectives

Learning about the landmark case of *Loving v. Virginia,* anti-miscegenation laws in the United States, historical inequity, and relating to current issues, rights, and laws.

Resources

Loving (2016), film directed by Jeff Nichols, with Oscar-nominated performance by Ruth Negga (available on Amazon Prime Video)

The Loving Story (2011), documentary film by Nancy Buirski (available through HBO)

Access to the website: www.lovingday.org

Please note that the film *Mr. and Mrs. Loving* (1996) is highly historically inaccurate and was not supported by Mrs. Loving.

Activities

1. Introduce concepts of race, segregation, anti-miscegenation, civil rights, interracial marriage, and other related terminology. Optional: do a pre-survey in the form of a mind map about concepts (either as a whole group on the board or within small groups and on a worksheet) to gauge what students know about these topics.

2. Ask students to visit www.lovingday.org, read the information under the tab "Learn," and take notes on the key dates and events from this historical account. Invite the students to click around on the interactive map to see how much of the country accepted or rejected interracial marriage by law.

3. Watch *Loving* (2016). Debrief questions: "What aspects of the *Loving v. Virginia* case were more vivid, through watching the film?" "What do you think about the laws that separated and segregated people due to race?"

4. Watch *The Loving Story* (2011). Debrief questions: "How does watching this film add more to your understanding or appreciation of this story and the case?" "What surprised you or intrigued you?" "What additional questions do you have about the case?"

5. Have students do a group project on one of the following or other related topic:

   a. Explore the US Census and give a report on the presence of multiracial individuals within your country, region, or neighborhood. How do these population counts reflect a relationship with the legalization of interracial marriage or the migration of peoples within your area?

   b. Research the case for interracial marriage by the American Civil Liberties Union (ACLU) and compare with another case by the ACLU (e.g., legalization of marriage for LGBTQ+ individuals). Explain the legal aspects of each case that are critical for understanding human, constitutional, and civil rights in this country. How is there still discrimination, despite there being legalization of interracial marriage?

    c. Create a script that is a shortened version of the *Loving* (2016) film and actual historical events. Discuss what you include, and why you consider these to be pivotal moments in the film and within history. Act out the script and film it, adding narration and any graphics or other visual images that can enhance learning for the audience.

6. Students share their projects in the form of a group presentation to the class, and answer any questions from the audience.

7. Summarize the group discussion: How does this exploration encourage you to be more involved in human rights or civil rights issues? What cause is of interest to you? What one immediate action can you take to make a difference in the world?

Extension: Advocacy and Activism

Write a letter or postcard to someone you know to share your thoughts on this issue and express your intentions to support or share information about a cause with others around you. Get involved with a program, action, or event to support the chosen cause.

Grade Level: 6–8, 9–12

Title: *"Multiracial Role Models"*

Subjects: *Art, Music, Economics, Current Events, Language Arts, Citizenship*

Educational Standards Addressed: ID.6-8.1 through ID.6-8.4, DI.6-8.7, DI.6-8.8, DI.6-8.9, JU.6-8.15, AC.6-8.20, ID.9-12.1 through ID.9-12.5, DI.9-12.6 through DI.9-12.10, JU.9-12.11 through JU.9-12.15, AC.9-12.16 through AC.9-12.20

Learning Objectives

Learning about the lives of multiracial artists and entrepreneurs who combine their artistic expression with community advocacy, education, and activism.

Resources

Access to internet articles, websites, and social media channels to research the artist contributions and the lives of multiracial artists and entrepreneurs, such as Louie Gong, Sonia Smith-Kang, and Maimouna Youssef.

Activities

1. Choose an independent multiracial artist/entrepreneur who also visibly supports a social cause with their efforts. Suggested for grades 6–8: Louie Gong or Sonia Smith-Kang. Suggested for grades 9–12: the aforementioned plus Maimouna Youssef.

2. Invite students to research the expression, talent, and craft of the artist and entrepreneur. Ask students to consider the following questions: "How does this individual infuse culture and their personal heritage into their work?" "How does this

individual demonstrate community activism and sharing awareness of and dialogue around social issues?" "How does supporting independent artists and entrepreneurs make a difference to the community?"

Overview of each artist:

- Louie Gong: artist, founder of Eighth Generation. Committed to supporting and advocating for a community of "Inspired Natives" rather than "Native inspired" and culturally appropriated art and consumer goods.

- Sonia Smith-Kang: parent, founder of Mixed Up Clothing, and co-founder of Culturas.us. Committed to the advancement of awareness and dialogue around multiracial identity, and cultural awareness through fashion and apparel, and community advocacy.

- Maimouna Youssef: vocal performer, songwriter, parent, and educator about self-empowerment, social issues, and the Black and Native experience. (Note that some lyrics are explicit, and the social issues she talks about require framing and debriefing for youth to understand and process.)

3. Create a digital collage about the artist, including snippets of quotes from magazines or video clips that capture the essence of their message. Share about their cultural and racial heritage so we can learn more about the overlapping identities that they hold. Share this in the form of a presentation to the class.

4. Create a presentation on yourself, inspired by the artist you have researched. What quotes, images, and videos would you include about yourself? Be sure to tell us about your own cultural and racial heritages and influences that affect your life. What is the message you want to share with the world? What is the cause you are inspired to pursue, through your own talents and efforts?

Afterword

THIS BOOK is an outgrowth of the author's existence as a multiracial individual, her intellect, her curiosity, and her determination to help us build a toolkit to navigate the challenging waters of children and their building of their racial/ethnic identities. Even though the multiracial community is expanding, the questions still get asked, such as "But what about the children?" Many of them are just fine, thank you very much. Some may not be, but that is true for self-perceived monoracial populations as well. In considering the but-what-about-the-children faux bia, the real question is "But what about society?" Too often, it picks at the epidermis of multiracial lives ("What are you?" "Gee, you don't look X!" "What race do you identify with most?" "Wow, I don't see it at all!"—this usually from strangers) to the extent that we develop a "rash," if you will. Then those same perpetrators point at us and squawk, "Look! Told you so! Half-breed children are *not* fine! Race mixing results in tragic beings!" (Apparently, this is especially true if the multiracial being is partially of African descent.) Childrearing must be done with thoughtfulness in any ethnic culture, but, because of society's tendency to scrutinize multiracial individuals more aggressively, a book like this one becomes essential. It is particularly important in a polarized, racially dualistic society such as the United States where things remain so very black and white.

My perspective aligns with that of this book: to consider offspring of interracial unions with regards to ways their journeys can be made safer, more confident, and more meaningful. Intentionality is critical. A big part of identity formation centers on what one wants to be called and what others think one ought to be called. Terminology will continue to be an issue vis-à-vis persons of mixed ethnic ancestry. For example, the idea of "race" is rejected by some as purely a construct of European American heteronormative patriarchy. On the other hand, terms such as "multiracial" and "monoracial" (for those who perceive themselves as having only one ethnic heritage) are deemed acceptable. Among mixed race individuals of the Asian diaspora, terms such as "Eurasian" are for people with one parent from Europe and one person from Asia, but often are used by persons who are Asian American and European American. Sometimes people who are White European American and Japanese or Japanese American call people who are mixed race Japanese or are Japanese Americans with African heritage "Blackanese," which, conversely, would make them "Whitanese." To complicate matters further, sometimes the term "Blasian" is used to describe persons who are of Asian/Asian American and African descent, which, conversely, would mean that White European American and Asian/Asian American mixtures are "Whasian." The mind boggles at the other implications. Lasians or Latinese for Latinx Asians? The term "Hapa" is used sociopolitically by mixed race Asian Americans, coming from the Hawaiian term for "half," which comes from the American English term for "half." In Japan, mixed race Japanese are referred to as *hāfu*. The term "biracial" often is used to describe individuals who are of White European/European American and African ancestries, but the term could refer to any individual who is composed of two races. I often meet monoracial people who express some version of this: "When you get right down to it, everybody's mixed, so what's the point of this biracial stuff?" Right. And all fruits have fructose, but they do not look or taste the same, and people react to them differently.

When my son was three, he played house at preschool with a White European American girl named Daisy. One day, she asked my son if I was his nanny. When he explained I was his mother, she asked if he was adopted. When he told her no again, she stated she could not play with him anymore, because she was White and he was not. A psychologist informed me that children's racial views are shaped usually by age four and by what they learn in the home. Children need to understand at an early age that, as Farzana Nayani states, there is more than one way to be. It centers them, and provides them with that "spirit of community and camaraderie" that Nayani addresses in this book.

When I was a child growing up in Kansas, despite the fact that I could talk with my parents about ethnicity and culture from age four, outside of our home existed a society that discouraged multiracial identity. Even today, I am aware of people who feel I should identify strongly with one ethnicity or another, not understanding that I am multiracial, not a hodgepodge of individual ethnicities. Many also question why Japanese culture is such a big part of my identity. Hmmm, could that have anything to do with the fact that I was reared by a native Japanese female immigrant and have remained close to that woman my entire life? Her imprint on me is the strongest force I have ever known. This is an example of how society attempts to suppress multiracial identity. Such circumstances support the need for this book. If only parents, teachers, school staff and administrators, health care professionals, and childcare providers had this resource when I was a child.

I wish we lived in a post-racial world, but we do not. Having books such as this one helps us navigate. I see progress, but also too many examples of backsliding that seem to have popped out of the 1920s. For example, in May 2019, I was walking on a Los Angeles university campus and had the misfortune of hearing five White European American male professors speaking (they did not see me). One of them stated with indignation, "I guess we're not special anymore because our ancestors didn't come from Africa." First, I thought about the term "come from Africa," as if Africans decided to immigrate to America, bought tickets, and boarded ships that carried them to the United States in a civilized fashion. Second, I was disgusted. Being Japanese, Black, Blackfoot Pikuni Native American, and Spanish with visible African heritage, I circled around and walked toward the gaggle of professors. I greeted them, and they responded with abundant and remarkable warmth. I wonder if anybody in their lives, particularly their Black students, could even picture them having the discussion I overheard.

The fact that many people, even those with potent moral compasses, still seem to have stereotypical ideas about what race is, who they think belongs to certain races, and how people of certain races behave galvanizes me to support this book. Identity must be nurtured, especially with regards to children. For multiracial individuals, an important part of identity is the blending of ethnicities and culture within one body. Just as members of governmentally standardized races—Asian, American Indian or Alaska Native, Black or African American, Hispanic or Latino, Native Hawaiian or Other Pacific Islander, White—may be proud of their racial heritages, guess what? So are multiracial people. They interact with monoracial people, but as themselves, as multiracial individuals. Being themselves does not magically emerge from their personas at age twenty-one; as this book notes, it is in the hearts of multiracial children; and something that we all should respect, cherish, and support.

A book like this one is critical to our united humanity. Whether we are teachers, parents, or friends, we all need tools to help the children in our lives cultivate their identity—not as we or society see it or want it to be, but with regards to how they see it and need it to be. Nayani's book guides us in the consideration of those tools, and in our efforts to apply those tools in helping us grow and helping children grow.

As a teaching society, yes, we consider all children. However, this book illustrates the fact that there is another dimension to consider for multiracial children. In education, we talk about the three

Rs—there is a fourth one: race. For multiracial children who do not fit into the standardized boxes of which teachers and parents seem to be most aware, multiracial differences and the identities they shape must not be suppressed. As you move forward, please allow this book to guide you in the journey of that discovery and recovery. Within family interactions, the multiracial individual experiences different cultures coalescing and colliding in ways that need support. Having read this book, you have the tools to make a difference. Onward.

—VELINA HASU HOUSTON, MFA, PhD
playwright and distinguished professor
Los Angeles, California
December 2019

Notes

Introduction

1 M. G. Vassanji, *No New Land* (Toronto: Emblem Editions, 1997).

2 Amy E. Ansell, "Color Blindness," in *Encyclopedia of Race, Ethnicity, and Society*, ed. Richard T. Schaefer (Thousand Oaks, CA: Sage, 2008), 320–22.

3 Gina Kamentsky and Julie Zammarchi, "Traffic Stop," YouTube video, 3:18, posted by StoryCorps, July 23, 2015, https://storycorps.org /animation/traffic-stop/.

4 "Social Justice at CCS," Children's Community School, accessed January 31, 2019, www.childrenscommunityschool.org/justice/.

Chapter 1

1 Karen R. Humes, Nicholas A. Jones, and Roberto R. Ramirez, "Overview of Race and Hispanic Origin: 2010," 2010 Census Briefs, United States Census Bureau, March 2011, accessed October 24, 2019, www .census.gov/prod/cen2010/briefs/c2010br-02.pdf.

2 "What Census Calls Us: A Historical Timeline," Pew Social Trends, accessed August 15, 2019, www.pewsocialtrends.org/interactives /multiracial-timeline/.

3 United States Census Bureau, American Fact Finder, accessed August 15, 2019, https://factfinder.census.gov/faces/nav/jsf/pages/index.xhtml.

4 "Appendix A: Revisions to the Standards for the Classification of Federal Data on Race and Ethnicity," National Center for Education Statistics, accessed October 22, 2019, https://nces.ed.gov/programs /handbook/data/pdf/Appendix_A.pdf.

5 Humes, Jones, and Ramirez, "Overview of Race and Hispanic Origin: 2010."

6 Nicholas A. Jones and Amy Symens Smith, "The Two or More Races Population: 2000," Census 2000 Brief, United States Census Bureau, 2001, accessed June 29, 2019, www.census.gov/prod/2001pubs/c2kbr01-6.pdf.

7 "2010 Census Shows America's Diversity," United States Census Bureau Newsroom Archive, accessed October 14, 2019, www.census.gov/newsroom/releases/archives/2010_census/cb11-cn125.html.

8 Humes, Jones, and Ramirez, "Overview of Race and Hispanic Origin: 2010."

9 Susan Saulny, "Census Data Presents Rise in Multiracial Population of Youths," New York Times, March 24, 2011, accessed August 15, 2019, www.nytimes.com/2011/03/25/us/25race.html.

10 Nicholas A. Jones and Jungmiwha Bullock, "The Two or More Races Population: 2010," 2010 Census Briefs, United States Census Bureau, September 2012, accessed October 5, 2019, www.census.gov/prod/cen2010/briefs/c2010br-13.pdf.

11 United States Census Bureau, 2017 American Community Survey Demographic and Housing Estimates, accessed October 15, 2019, https://data.census.gov/cedsci/table?d=ACS%205-Year%20Estimates%20Data%20Profiles&table=DP05&tid=ACSDP5Y2017.DP05&lastDisplayedRow=50.

12 Brittany Rico, Rose M. Kreider, and Lydia Anderson, "Growth in Interracial and Interethnic Married-Couple Households," United States Census Bureau, July 9, 2018, accessed June 29, 2019, www.census.gov/library/stories/2018/07/interracial-marriages.html.

13 Loving Day, accessed August 21, 2019, http://lovingday.org.

14 "Census Profile, 2016 Census," Statistics Canada, June 18, 2019, accessed August 15, 2019, www12.statcan.gc.ca/census-recensement/2016/dp-pd/prof/index.cfm.

15 Douglas Todd, "Vancouver Has Highest Ratio of Mixed Couples. But Victoria, Kelowna Real Surprises," Vancouver Sun, June 17, 2014, accessed August 14, 2019, https://vancouversun.com/news/staff-blogs/metro-van-has-most-mixed-couples-in-canada.

16 Nazima Walji, "'We Were Just Gawked At': Mixed-Race Families Common in Canada but Still Face Challenges," CBC News, November 3, 2017, accessed August 14, 2019, www.cbc.ca/news/canada/mixed-race-families-in-canada-1.4376379.

17 Sandra Winn Tutwiler, *Mixed-Race Youth and Schooling: The Fifth Minority* (New York: Routledge, 2016).

18 Ramona E. Douglass, "The Evolution of the Multiracial Movement," in *Multiracial Child Resource Book: Living Complex Identities,* eds. Maria P. P. Root and Matt Kelley (Seattle: MAVIN Foundation, 2003), 12–17.

Chapter 2

1 Cory Turner, "Why All Parents Should Talk with Their Kids about Social Identity," NPR Morning Edition, October 7, 2019, accessed October 20, 2019, www.npr.org/2019/10/08/767205198/the-things -parents-dont-talk-about-with-their-kids-but-should.

2 Mitch R. Hammer, *The Intercultural Development Inventory (IDI v5)* (Olney, MD: IDI, 2019).

3 Milton Bennett, "A Developmental Approach to Training Intercultural Sensitivity," special issue on Intercultural Training, *International Journal of Intercultural Relations* 10, no. 2 (1986): 179–86, https://doi .org/10.1016/0147-1767(86)90005-2.

4 Teaching Tolerance, accessed August 14, 2019, www.tolerance.org/.

5 "Let's Talk! Discussing Race, Racism and Other Difficult Topics with Students," Teaching Tolerance, accessed August 14, 2019, www .tolerance.org/magazine/publications/lets-talk.

Chapter 3

1 Elizabeth Kleinrock, Teach and Transform, personal correspondence, October 29, 2019.

2 National Institutes of Health, "Stereotype Threat," US Department of Health and Human Services, accessed July 15, 2019, https://diversity .nih.gov/sociocultural-factors/stereotype-threat.

3 C. M. Steele and J. Aronson, "Stereotype Threat and the Intellectual Test Performance of African Americans," *Journal of Personality and Social Psychology* 69, no. 5 (1995): 797–811.

4 E. J. R. David, *Brown Skin, White Minds: Filipino-American Postcolonial Psychology* (Charlotte, NC: Information Age Publishing, 2013).

5 Dr. Sarah Gaither, personal correspondence, October 25, 2019.

Chapter 4

1 Farzana Nayani, *Being All of Me: A Handbook for Teachers and Parents of Multiracial, Multiethnic, and Transracially Adopted Children* (Los Angeles: Multiracial Americans of Southern California, 2017).

2 Farzana Nayani, "Family Communication Patterns of Multiethnic Filipino-American Youth in Hawai'i," in *Multiethnicity & Multiethnic Families: Development, Identity, and Resilience,* eds. Hamilton McCubbin et al. (Honolulu: Le'a Publications, 2010), 199–224.

3 Charmaine L. Wijeyesinghe, Pat Griffin, and Barbara Love, "Racism Curriculum Design," in *Teaching for Diversity and Social Justice: A Sourcebook,* eds. Maurianne Adams, Lee Anne Bell, and Pat Griffin (New York: Routledge, 1997), 82–109.

4 Maria P. P. Root, "Bill of Rights for Racially Mixed People," in *Multiracial Child Resource Book: Living Complex Identities,* eds. Maria P. P. Root and Matt Kelley (Seattle: MAVIN Foundation, 2003), 32.

5 Kip Fulbeck, *Part Asian, 100% Hapa* (San Francisco: Chronicle Books, 2010).

6 Curtiss Takada Rooks, personal correspondence, October 25, 2019.

7 Jean S. Phinney, "Stages of Ethnic Identity in Minority Group Adolescents," *Journal of Early Adolescence* 9 (1989): 34–49.

8 W. S. Carlos Poston, "The Biracial Identity Development Model: A Needed Addition," *Journal of Counseling and Development* 69 (1990): 152–55.

9 J. Fuji Collins, "Biracial Japanese American Identity: An Evolving Process," *Cultural Diversity and Ethnic Minority Psychology* 6 (2000): 115–33.

10 Reginald G. Daniel, "Black and White Identity in the New Millennium," in *The Multiracial Experience: Racial Borders as the New Frontier,* ed. Maria P. P. Root (Thousand Oaks, CA: Sage, 1996), 121–39.

11 Kerry Ann Rockquemore and David L. Brunsma, *Beyond Black: Biracial Identity in America* (Thousand Oaks, CA: Sage, 2002).

12 Maria P. P. Root, "Resolving 'Other' Status: Identity Development of Biracial Individuals," in *Diversity and Complexity in Feminist Therapy,* eds. Laura S. Brown and Maria P. P. Root (New York: Haworth, 1990), 185–205.

13 Kristen A. Renn, "Research on Biracial and Multiracial Identity Development: Overview and Synthesis," in *New Directions for Student Services*

123 (Fall 2008), 13–21, accessed September 17, 2019, https://msu .edu/~renn/RennNewDirectionsMR2008.pdf.

14 Charmaine L. Wijeyesinghe, "The Intersectional Model of Multiracial Identity Integrating Multiracial Identity Theories and Intersectional Perspectives on Social Identity," in *New Perspectives on Racial Identity Development: Integrating Emerging Frameworks,* 2nd ed., eds. Charmaine L. Wijeyesinghe and Bailey W. Jackson (New York: NYU Press, 2012), 81–107, accessed September 19, 2019, www.academia. edu/31140509/The_Intersectional_Model_of_Multiracial_Identity _Integrating_Multiracial_Identity_Theories_and_Intersectional _Perspectives_on_Social_Identity.

Chapter 5

1 *Time,* "The New Face of America," *Time* magazine, November 1993.

2 *Time,* November 18, 1993, *Time* magazine cover, "The New Face of America," accessed July 15, 2019, http://content.time.com/time /covers/0,16641,19931118,00.html.

3 Lise Funderburg, "The Changing Face of America," *National Geographic,* October 2013, accessed July 15, 2019, www.nationalgeographic .com/magazine/2013/10/changing-face-america.

4 *National Geographic,* "Black and White," *National Geographic,* April 2018.

5 Derald Wing Sue, *Microaggressions in Everyday Life: Race, Gender, and Sexual Orientation* (Hoboken, NJ: John Wiley & Sons, 2010).

6 Lindsay Pérez Huber and Daniel Solorzano, "Racial Microaggressions as a Tool for Critical Race Research," *Race, Ethnicity, and Education* 18, no. 3 (May 2015): 297–320, http://dx.doi.org/10.1080/13613324 .2014.994173.

7 Chimamanda Ngozi Adichie, "The Danger of a Single Story," TED Talk, October 7, 2009, accessed October 11, 2019, www.youtube .com/watch?v=D9Ihs24Izeg.

8 Marc P. Johnston and Kevin L. Nadal, "Multiracial Microaggressions: Exposing Monoracism in Everyday Life and Clinical Practice," in *Microaggressions and Marginality: Manifestations, Dynamics, and Impact,* ed. Derald Wing Sue (Hoboken, NJ: John Wiley & Sons, 2010), 123–44.

9 Eric Hamako, "Recognizing and Remedying Monoracism in Antiracist Education," Global Mixed Race: Critical Mixed Race Studies, DePaul University, Chicago, 2014.

10 Associated Press, "Interracial Couple Denied Marriage License," October 15, 2009, accessed July 14, 2019, www.nbcnews.com/id/33332436/ns/us_news-life/t/interracial-couple-denied-marriage-license/#.XVaOJC2ZP04.

11 Michael Genhart, *Ouch! Moments: When Words Are Used in Hurtful Ways* (Washington, DC: Magination Press, 2016).

12 Farzana Nayani, *Being All of Me: A Handbook for Teachers and Parents of Multiracial, Multiethnic, and Transracially Adopted Children* (Los Angeles: Multiracial Americans of Southern California, 2017).

13 Farzana Nayani, "Family Communication Patterns of Multiethnic Filipino-American Youth in Hawai'i," in *Multiethnicity & Multiethnic Families: Development, Identity, and Resilience,* eds. Hamilton McCubbin et al. (Honolulu: Le'a Publications, 2010), 199–224.

14 Kimberlé Crenshaw, "Mapping the Margins: Intersectionality, Identity Politics, and Violence against Women of Color," *Stanford Law Review* 43, no. 6 (July 1991): 1241–99.

15 Patricia Hill Collins and Sirma Bilge, *Intersectionality* (Malden, MA: Polity Press, 2016).

16 Kelly Faye Jackson and Gina Miranda Samuels, *Multiracial Cultural Attunement* (Washington, DC: NASW Press, 2019).

17 Genevieve Rajewski, "Pulling Back the Curtain on DNA Ancestry Tests," TuftsNow, January 26, 2018, accessed October 25, 2019, https://now.tufts.edu/articles/pulling-back-curtain-dna-ancestry-tests.

18 Aeriel Ashlee, "Can a DNA Ancestry Test Tell Me Who I Am? Multiple Perspectives on Direct-to-Consumer Ancestry Testing and Implications for Higher Education," National Conference on Race and Ethnicity (NCORE), May 29, 2019.

Chapter 6

1 Anderson Cooper, "Inside the AC360 Doll Study," YouTube video, 5:27, posted by CNN, May 17, 2010, www.youtube.com/watch?v=DYCz1ppTjiM.

2 "Social Justice Standards: A Professional Development Facilitator Guide," Teaching Tolerance, 2018, accessed August 14, 2019, www.tolerance.org/professional-development/facilitator-guides.

3 "Social Justice Standards: A Framework for Anti-Bias Education," Teaching Tolerance, accessed August 14, 2019, www.tolerance.org /frameworks/social-justice-standards.

4 "Social Justice Standards: The Teaching Tolerance Anti-Bias Framework," Teaching Tolerance, accessed August 14, 2019, www.tolerance .org/professional-development/social-justice-standards-the-teaching -tolerance-antibias-framework.

Chapter 7

1 Premila D'Sa, "A Canadian University Asks Black Student to Prove Minorities Exist on Campus," *VICE,* November 22, 2017, accessed August 4, 2019, www.vice.com/en_us/article/pa3nb7/a-canadian -university-asks-black-student-to-prove-minorities-exist-on-campus.

2 Andy Riemer, personal correspondence, November 4, 2019.

3 "Join the Harvard Graduate School of Education's MIXED (Multiracial Students eXchanging and Encouraging Dialogue) Student Group," February 1, 2019, accessed December 10, 2019, https://hls .harvard.edu/join-the-harvard-graduate-school-of-educations-mixed -multiracial-students-exchanging-and-encouraging-dialogue-student -group/.

4 NASPA MultiRacial Knowledge Community, Facebook page, accessed August 4, 2019, www.facebook.com/pg/NASPAMRKC/about/?ref =page_internal.

5 "Social Justice Retreats," Oregon State University, accessed August 4, 2019, https://dce.oregonstate.edu/retreat.

6 "Racial Aikido," Oregon State University, accessed November 30, 2019, https://experience.oregonstate.edu/resources/racial-aikido.

7 Charlene Martinez, personal correspondence, August 5, 2019.

8 "Call for Nominations: Undergraduate University Awards," University of Maryland, January 17, 2019, accessed August 4, 2019, https:// studentaffairs.umd.edu/news/call-for-nominations-undergraduate -university-awards.

9 Mixed Alumni Association, UCLA, accessed August 5, 2019, https:// alumni.ucla.edu/alumni-networks/mixed-alumni-association/.

10 "Conferences," Critical Mixed Race Studies, accessed August 4, 2019, https://criticalmixedracestudies.com/conferences.

11 "About," MidWest Mixed, accessed August 4, 2019, www.midwest
   mixed.com/about.

12 Hapa Japan, accessed August 4, 2019, https://hapajapan.com.

13 "About," Hapa-palooza: A Celebration of Mixed Roots Arts and Ideas,
   accessed August 4, 2019, www.hapapalooza.com/about.

14 Dr. Sarah Gaither, personal correspondence, October 25, 2019.

15 Paul Pringle and Adam Elmahrek, "Native American Minority Con-
   tracts Are under Scrutiny as Officials Vow Strict Enforcement," *Los
   Angeles Times,* July 2, 2019, accessed August 4, 2019, www.latimes.
   com/local/lanow/la-me-ln-native-american-minority-contracts-
   cherokee-20190702-story.html.

16 Tanya Katerí Hernández, *Multiracials and Civil Rights: Mixed-Race
   Stories of Discrimination* (New York: NYU Press, 2018).

Chapter 8

1 Diana T. Sanchez, "How Do Forced-Choice Dilemmas Affect Multiracial People? The Role of Identity Autonomy and Public Regard in
   Depressive Symptoms," *Journal of Applied Social Psychology* 40 (2010):
   1657–77.

2 Richard Alba, "There's a Big Problem with How the Census Measures Race," *Washington Post,* February 6, 2018, accessed August 15,
   2019, www.washingtonpost.com/news/monkey-cage/wp/2018/02/06
   /theres-a-big-problem-with-how-the-census-measures-race
   /?noredirect=on.

3 *Race in Medicine: A Dangerous Prescription,* video (Los Angeles:
   Multiracial Americans of Southern California, 2012).

4 Athena Asklipiadis, personal correspondence, August 6, 2019.

5 Geneva Gay, *Culturally Responsive Teaching: Theory, Research, and
   Practice,* 3rd ed. (New York: Teachers College Press, 2018).

Appendix A

Gene Batiste, ed., *Diversity Work in Independent Schools: The Practice and
   the Practitioner* (Washington, DC: National Association of Independent Schools, 2017).

The BIPOC Project, accessed October 1, 2019, www.thebipocproject.org.

E. J. R. David and Sumie Okazaki, "Activation and Automaticity of Colonial Mentality," *Journal of Applied Social Psychology* 40, no. 4 (April 1, 2010): 850, doi:10.1111/j.1559-1816.2010.00601.x.

Glossary, Racial Equity Tools, accessed October 9, 2019, www.racial equitytools.org/glossary.

Eric Hamako, "Recognizing and Remedying Monoracism in Anti-racist Education," Global Mixed Race: Critical Mixed Race Studies, DePaul University, Chicago, 2014.

"Identity Covering in the Workplace: Definition, Examples & Implications," video, Study.com, accessed October 28, 2019, https://study .com/academy/lesson/identity-covering-in-the-workplace-definition -examples-implications.html.

Merriam-Webster dictionary, www.merriam-webster.com/dictionary/, accessed October 28, 2019.

Farzana Nayani, *Being All of Me: A Handbook for Teachers and Parents of Multiracial, Multiethnic, and Transracially Adopted Children* (Los Angeles: Multiracial Americans of Southern California, 2017).

"'Racial Impostor Syndrome': Here Are Your Stories," NPR Code Switch, January 17, 2018, accessed October 25, 2019, www.npr .org/sections/codeswitch/2018/01/17/578386796/racial-impostor -syndrome-here-are-your-stories.

C. M. Steele and J. Aronson, "Stereotype Threat and the Intellectual Test Performance of African Americans," *Journal of Personality and Social Psychology* 69, no. 5 (1995): 797–811.

Stella Ting-Toomey and Leeva C. Chung, *Understanding Intercultural Communication,* 2nd ed. (Oxford: Oxford University Press, 2012).

Francis Wardle and Marta I. Cruz-Janzen, *Meeting the Needs of Multiethnic and Multiracial Children in Schools* (Boston: Pearson Education, 2004).

Charmaine L. Wijeyesinghe, Pat Griffin, and Barbara Love, "Racism Curriculum Design," in *Teaching for Diversity and Social Justice: A Sourcebook,* eds. Maurianne Adams, Lee Anne Bell, and Pat Griffin (New York: Routledge, 1997), 82–109.

Appendix B

1 "Social Justice Standards: A Professional Development Facilitator Guide," 2018.

Index

family *(continued)*
    multifaith, 114–115
    multiracial identity in, 109–117
    resources, 116–117
    siblings and other members,
        109–111
fashion, recommended resources, 193
fear, talking about race and, 30, 41
festivals, recommended resources, 192
Filipino, US Census, 17
Filipinx, 203
films, multiracial issues-based,
    193–194
FMMI (Factor Model of Multiracial
    Identity), 89
FOCS (Families of Color Seattle), 180
forced choice, 154, 203
forms
    choice of racial identity on,
        168–171
    multiracial identity on health,
        171–172
fractions
    biracial identity in United States
        Census, 17
    multiracial descriptions using,
        26–27
free colored males and females, US
    Census, 17
free white females, US Census, 17
free white males, US Census, 17
friendships, multiracial identity and,
    113–114
Fulbeck, Kip, 80–82
functional integrative identity, 87

G

Gaddy, Levonne, 180
Gaither, Dr. Sarah, 64, 155
games, recommended resources,
    186–187
gatekeeper phenomenon, 83–85
Gay, Dr. Geneva, 174
genealogy, DNA ancestry testing for,
    115–116

general student experience, colleges/
    universities, 150–151
general workplace dynamics, career,
    163, 165
Gong, Louis, 233–234
grades, schoolchildren. *see* lesson plans
Guamanian, US Census, 18

H

Hafu, 25, 236
Hafu2Hafu, 137, 139
Halagao, Dr. Patricia E., 122–123
half-breed, 26
Hapa identity
    definition of, 203
    mixed Asian heritage, 236
    as multiracial descriptor, 25
    overview of, 80–82
Hapa Japan Conference, 150
hapa.me (Fulbeck), 137–138
Hathaway, Patsy, 7
Hawaiians
    multiracial population study of,
        3–4
    US Census, 17
healing, recommended resources,
    196–197
health, multiracial identity and,
    171–174
Helms, Dr. Gabrielle, 2
help, for microaggressions, 106–107
heritage
    DNA ancestry testing for, 115–116,
        158
    family dynamics and, 111–112
    Racial Dialogue Readiness and, 42
    using fractions to describe
        multiracial heritage, 26
Hernández, Tanya Katerí, 161
hiding, from microaggression, 106
Hindu, US Census, 17
Hispanic ethnic group
    choice of racial identity on
        forms, 170
    interracial unions in US, 22

interracial unions *(continued)*
    Supreme Court ruling in favor of,
      180, 195
    US Census statistics, 22
intersectionality
    career considerations, 153
    co-working spaces and, 160
    definition of, 205
    in legal cases of discrimination,
      162
    multidimensionality and, 112–113
    multifaith families and, 114
isolation
    consciousness of race and, 48–49
    multiracial microaggressions and,
      98–99
    overcoming sense of, 176

J

Japanese, US Census, 17
Johnston-Guerrero (Johnston), Dr.
    Marc, 98
Jones, Nicholas, 21
justice
    3-5 grade-level outcomes, 216–217
    6-8 grade-level outcomes, 218–219
    9-12 grade-level outcomes, 221
    K-2 grade-level outcomes,
      214–215
    as social justice anchor standard,
      128–129

K

Kleinrock, Liz, 53
Korean, US Census, 17

L

Lam, Kin Wah, 93
Landau, Alex, 7
Latinas and Latinos of Mixed Ancestry
    (LOMA), 170
Latino ethnic group, 20, 170
Latinx
    dating issues, 113
    employee resource groups, 154

ethnicity examples, 202
imposter syndrome and, 58
proving racial legitimacy, 71
student groups on campuses, 144
US Census and, 170
leadership, in multiracial business, 159
Leopardo, Nicole, 144
lesson plans
    3-5 grade-level, 224–226
    6-8, 9-12 grade-level, 137–139
    6-8 grade-level, 227–229,
      233–234
    9-12 grade-level, 227–234
    K-2 grade-level, 224–226
    K-3 grade-level, 134–136
    K-5 grade level, 132–133
LGBTQ+, 154, 206
Logia, Jenifer, 148
LOMA (Latinas and Latinos of Mixed
    Ancestry), 170
Lopez, Thomas, 170
Loving (2016) film, 231–232
Loving Day Conference, 180
Loving Day conference, 150
"Loving Day Lives" lesson plan (grades
    9-12), 230–232
The Loving Story (2011) film, 231
Loving v. Virginia (1967), 22, 150

M

MALDEF (Mexican American
    Legal Defense and Educational
    Fund), 24
marginalization
    career considerations, 153
    Conscious Cultivation of Identity
      model and, 48–49
    definition of, 206
    hiding true race due to, 24
    intersectionality/
      multidimensionality and,
      112–113
    racially driven experiences of, 33
    social stratification and, 3
    stereotype threat and, 55

"Our Unique Families" lesson plan
(grades K-5), 224–226
outcomes, grade-level. *see* Social
Justice Standards, outcomes
ownership, multiracial business, 159

P

Pacific Islanders, US Census, 18
Parent Teacher Associations (PTAs),
179
parenting. *see also* action, advocacy
and community-building
differences between siblings, 109
exposure and reinforcement of
culture, 72–74
family dynamics and, 112
how to talk about race/
multiraciality, 63–68
intention to face race/teach
multiracial identity, 82–83
racial identity self-reflection
questionnaire, 89–90
recommended resources, 187
role in modeling racial identity,
59–60
Part Asian, 100% Hapa (Fulbeck),
137–138
Part Hawaiian, US Census, 17
pathologizing multiracial identity/
experiences, 103–104
People Colors crayons, 120–122
People of Color (POC)
BIPOC. *see* Black, Indigenous,
and Other People of Color
(BIPOC)
definition of, 207
discrimination against, 162
institutional racism and, 210
performing arts, recommended
resources, 192–193
performing identity, 57–58, 207
Pew Research Center, 23–25
phenotype, 74–76, 207
pluralistic identity, 87
podcasts, recommended resources, 192

polarization, 35–37, 43–44, 79–80
policies, choice of racial identity on
forms, 168–171
political events, 42
post-racial society, 94, 208
power dynamics
adult readiness to talk race and,
10, 42
affect on individual or groups,
38–39
communication about, 48–49
prejudice, classroom education
on, 129
prescription drugs, multiracial identity
and, 171–173
privacy issues, DNA ancestry testing,
115
privilege
adult readiness to talk race and, 10
definition of, 208
experiences of those without, 33
intersectionality/
multidimensionality
impacting, 112–113
lighter skinned siblings and, 109
looking away from race tied to,
32–33
positioning of multiracial person
to gain, 59
Racial Dialogue Readiness and, 42
recommended resources, 190–191
professional associations, resources,
195–196
protean identity, 87
PTAs (Parent Teacher Associations),
179
Puerto Rican, US Census, 17
Pura Vida, bone marrow registry, 173

Q

Quadroon, 17, 208

R

race
definition of, 16, 208

About the Author

FARZANA NAYANI is a multiethnic author raising multiracial children. She is a passionate advocate and educator regarding the understanding of culture and race within organizations, schools, and the community. She holds a master's degree in communications and management from the University of Hawai'i at Mānoa and the esteemed East–West Center, as well as a bachelor of education and a bachelor of arts in psychology and English from the University of British Columbia. As a certified teacher and former TESOL instructor, Nayani has focused on bridging understanding across cultural differences throughout her entire career.

In her current work as a diversity, equity, and inclusion consultant and intercultural trainer, Nayani has conducted research, workshops, and curriculum design on cross-cultural topics for two decades. Her work has appeared in *Forbes, DiversityInc, L.A. Parent,* the *Smithsonian,* and on NPR. She is on the advisory board of Multiracial Americans of Southern California, is a part of the CAUSE Leadership Network, advises for the National Association of Asian American Professionals (NAAAP), and is coaching faculty for the Diversity, Equity, and Inclusion Coaching Center at The Forum on Workplace Inclusion. More about Nayani can be found at www.farzananayani.com.

About North Atlantic Books

North Atlantic Books (NAB) is an independent, nonprofit publisher committed to a bold exploration of the relationships between mind, body, spirit, and nature. Founded in 1974, NAB aims to nurture a holistic view of the arts, sciences, humanities, and healing. To make a donation or to learn more about our books, authors, events, and newsletter, please visit www.northatlanticbooks.com.

North Atlantic Books is the publishing arm of the Society for the Study of Native Arts and Sciences, a 501(c)(3) nonprofit educational organization that promotes cross-cultural perspectives linking scientific, social, and artistic fields. To learn how you can support us, please visit our website.